AFTER THE DEATH OF LITERATURE

AFTER THE DEATH OF LITERATURE

Richard B. Schwartz

Southern Illinois University Press
Carbondale and Edwardsville

Copyright © 1997 by the Board of Trustees,
Southern Illinois University
All rights reserved
Printed in the United States of America
00 99 98 97 4 3 2 1

Library of Congress Cataloging-in-Publication Data

Schwartz, Richard B.
After the death of literature / Richard B. Schwartz.
p.   cm.
Includes bibliographical references and index.
1. Criticism.   2. Literature—History and
criticism—Theory, etc.
I. Title.
PN81.S243   1997
801'.95—dc21   96-53317
ISBN 0-8093-2136-X (alk. paper)   CIP

The paper used in this publication meets the minimum
requirements of American National Standard for Information
Sciences—Permanence of Paper for Printed Library Materials,
ANSI Z39.48-1984. ♾

For Judith and Jonathan, Kirsten,
Katharine, and Caroline,
with my thanks for all of their love and help

CONTENTS

Acknowledgments *ix*

Introduction *1*

1. Johnson: The Writer as Critic *10*

2. Canons and Culture Wars *25*

3. Are Addison and Steele Dead? *60*

4. Vaticide for Fun and Profit *78*

5. The Two Kants *93*

6. The War Between the Straw Men *113*

7. Quo Vadis? *135*

Bibliography *161*

Index *175*

ACKNOWLEDGMENTS

Some of the material in chapter 1 originally appeared in an essay, "Samuel Johnson: The Professional Writer as Critic," included in a 1987 volume edited by Prem Nath, entitled *Fresh Reflections on Samuel Johnson: Essays in Criticism*. I am grateful to Whitston for permission to reprint. I am also particularly grateful to Tracey Sobol-Hill for shepherding the manuscript through the reviewing processes at Southern Illinois University Press. Dorothy Brown, Richard Stites, and John Samples all provided encouragement at crucial times. Finally, I would like to take this opportunity to pay tribute to my first mentor, the late Robert L. Haig, and my friend and colleague, the late Jean Hagstrum, whose early account of Johnson's criticism continues to endure, and to thank the late Donald Greene for setting an ongoing example of courage under fire and demonstrating the consummate use of the twin Johnsonian weapons of hard fact and common sense. As always, I wish to express special thanks to my son Jonathan and my beloved wife, Judith, from whom I always learn and who always believes.

INTRODUCTION

Like most individuals involved in the study of literature, I have been interested in the critical and theoretical developments that gained momentum in the 1970s and stimulated some aspects of the culture wars of the 1980s. For some time I have wondered what the response of Samuel Johnson might be to those events. In some cases his responses are easily predicted; in others they must be inferred. Johnson, as the greatest literary critic since Aristotle, would, I assume, have a number of interesting reflections to offer, some deliciously polemical, some deeply thoughtful and suggestive.

It would be interesting, I thought, to observe the culture wars from Johnson's perspective, asking the key questions: what should we read, how should we read it, and why should we read it? However, I believe that the culture wars—certainly in their most brash and stereotypical form—are by now slowly coming to a close and new developments are emerging. What would Johnson think of those newer prospects, and what advice might he proffer for those at work in the period after the occurrence that Alvin Kernan has characterized as the death of literature?

I should say at the outset that I believe that the stakes of the wars and the postures of the combatants have been much exaggerated. One thing that has been particularly exaggerated is the manner in which the intensity of the conflict and the intensity of the feelings concerning the conflict have been presented. The orchestration and staging of the battles have been superb. What we have witnessed, I will argue later, is a battle between straw men, carefully constructed by the combatants to sustain a pattern of polarization that could be exploited to provide continuing professional advancement. While that point might sound harsh, I am hardly the first to make it. Its articulation has, in many ways, been inevitable. Whenever one looks at the unnecessary perpetuation of a war, one is forced to ask who it is that gains by that perpetuation. Many others, closer than myself to the actual fray, have made the Pogoesque point that, having met the enemy, we now realize that that enemy is ourselves, particularly in our professionalization of literary activity and our participation in the economy generated by academic structures and academic reward systems. Rapprochement is less interesting than battle, middle ground somehow less attractive than the estates on the edge.

For many of us the problem is less with the outlines of current theoretical practices than with the needlessly complex language in which the practices are embodied and the exaggerated claims of originality that attend them. The claims of originality (required, it would seem, by the economy of the profession) are hardly crucial to the intellectual success of the practices.

In the recently published *Johns Hopkins Guide to Literary Theory and Criticism*, for example, Hunter Cadzow writes of New Historicism, pointing to the concerns of Greenblatt and others with regard to two orientations that the advocates of New Historicism have been anxious to move beyond: first, the consigning of texts to an autonomous aesthetic realm à la the New Criticism and, second, the notion that texts (Renaissance texts in this case) mirrored a "unified and coherent world-view that was held by a whole population, or at least by an entire literate class" (Groden and Kreiswirth, p. 535).

Who really took these views seriously, particularly as late as the early 1980s? Crane struggled against the tendencies of New Criticism over forty years ago, and much of the great postwar historical scholarship—certainly that in the eighteenth century—disregards the "autonomous aesthetic realm" idea entirely. New Criticism—in the larger scheme of things—was principally a classroom tool. As to the notion of a "coherent world-view," Tillyard's *Elizabethan World Picture* is over fifty years old, and it was used as a catechism rather than as adult theology as long ago as the 1950s.

In my own field, Paul Fussell's *Rhetorical World of Augustan Humanism: Ethics and Imagery from Swift to Burke* (1965) has long been criticized for devoting too much attention to intellectual and cultural coherence exemplified by commonalities among writers and too little to the disjunctions between them. Indeed, after Howard Weinbrot's work, many now would not even use the word *Augustan* in connection with the English eighteenth century.

Introduction

What has been most striking to me (I assume it would be equally striking to Johnson) is the extent to which charges and countercharges have been made that bear little relation to reality and the extent to which "reality" has been characterized in ways that bear little or no relation to actual experience. (Johnson's possible explanation: "That which is strange is delightful, and a pleasing error is not willingly detected" [*Journey, Yale Edition of the Works of Samuel Johnson*, 9:31].) Let me give an example. I recently received a university newsletter designed to apprise me of the many good things occurring these days at one of my alma maters. The newsletter included a proud account of the thought and activity of one bright young professor of American literature who was interested in challenging the traditional construction of the literary canon. His posture was a familiar one:

> Literary canons are made by those with access to the institutions that produce and reproduce literary taste, such as textbook publishers, journals, schools and universities.... Their tendency has been to choose from amongst their own: northeastern white protestant males from more or less privileged backgrounds. ("Rethinking the Canon," p. 5)

Why continue to lash the corpse of *this* horse, I thought. There is a kernel of truth to it, but no more than that. The more I considered it, however, the more I realized that the statement was not simply a stereotypical one of the sort we have all come to expect, but a grossly inaccurate one that would not have been taken seriously a generation ago. I could hear the opposition voices in the background, rising to the defense of the young revisionist, claiming that the earlier generation would have been unimpressed with the statement because that generation was hopelessly benighted—a group of hegemonic troglodytes who consistently failed to see the bitter, oppressive realities of the literary and cultural economy because of the obvious fact that it was constructed with the singular purpose of sustaining their hegemony. No, I thought, it would not have been taken seriously because it was historically inaccurate and did not square with the lessons of the 1950s and 1960s classroom.

Who are these northeastern white Protestant males? Willa Cather? Ernest Hemingway? F. Scott Fitzgerald? William Faulkner? John Steinbeck? William Styron? James Agee? James T. Farrell? Those were the writers my American literature teacher foisted upon me and my classmates thirty years ago.

Perhaps we must restrict this to *nineteenth*-century America; then we will find that good old northeastern WASP male establishment. Emily Dickinson? That staid and dour bastion of conservatism, Walt Whitman? All right, then—Melville, Hawthorne, Emerson, and Thoreau. I regret to say that while my teachers treated Melville with a certain degree of reverence (though criticizing what were starkly called his "potboilers"), Hawthorne was charged with an ahistorical falsifying of the realities of puritan America, Emerson was celebrated more for his countercultural inclinations than his ties with any eastern establishment, and the departmental heart's darling was Thoreau. Why? Because it was felt that less respect should be accorded those writers who were more regional and time-bound. "Local colorist" was not a positive term; it would be equatable now with something like "writer of genre fiction."

The norm was more a Johnsonian one. Who has pleased many and pleased long? Whose work transcends its time and place? Answer: Thoreau, who was much more than a New England writer; Thoreau influenced Gandhi. And, of course, Thoreau influenced Martin Luther King Jr. The point that was driven home again and again was that Thoreau was talking about much more than Walden Pond: he was talking about America; he was talking about the human spirit; he was talking about society; he was talking about human development. Thoreau went to jail for his beliefs. Thoreau challenged established behaviors. "What are you doing out *there*, Waldo?"

Some of my education might have reflected a midwestern chauvinism in my instructors (one *-ism* that seems to have escaped the ire of the cultural warriors). Far from inflicting upon us a northeastern WASP male mind-set, our instructors reminded us of the cultural importance of Chicago, most notably in architecture, but in literature as well. I do not believe that this can be attributed to cultural commonality, that is, the desire to maintain a closed club of like-minded mandarins: Chicago above all and the rest be damned. Frank Lloyd Wright, after all, was not what Johnson would have considered a clubbable man. Carl Sandburg and James T. Farrell were too popular for most academic clubs, and Saul Bellow was anything but a WASP.

One of the first documents pressed into our youthful hands was

Introduction

Philip Rahv's paleface and redskin essay, arguing not for a northeastern WASP male tradition but for a double vision that paired the introspective, guilt-ridden, European East with the physical and cultural expansiveness of the American West. The West had attracted D. H. Lawrence (as well as Georgia O'Keeffe and Ansel Adams), we were told, and we were promptly handed R. W. B. Lewis's *American Adam* and Henry Nash Smith's *Virgin Land*. Faulkner was taught from the point of view of the Turner hypothesis as well as within the context of southern culture and experimental narrative.

We were also introduced to the writings of public intellectuals. Paul Goodman was a mainstay, and we worried over Dwight Macdonald's "Masscult and Midcult" article, attacking him for (among other things) his pathetic ignorance of rock music. Macdonald was the Allan Bloom of our generation, haughty in his disdain for many of the things we liked. Jonathan Kozol was just getting under way; we read his fiction. We were particularly taken with writers who were in (but not entirely of) the universities, New York intellectuals often, but Jews rather than WASPs—Trilling especially, and Irving Howe, but also Kazin, whose *On Native Grounds* was required reading.

I *do* remember being struck by the sharp distinction drawn between serious and popular writing, but the teaching of African American writers was done routinely and with no great fanfare. We were forced to read Ralph Ellison; Harlan Ellison we would have to discover on our own. We were forced to read James Baldwin; James M. Cain we had to read on our own time.

The pigeonholing of writers was sometimes encountered, but it was usually by genre or subject rather than by race, religion, gender, or mailing address. We were much taken, for example, with Nathanael West, who was categorized as a "California novelist." And who is to say that that is not fair? Who *was* West? Nathan Wallenstein Weinstein, born in New York, 1902? Or Pep West, western screenwriter and novelist?

I have to admit that I think of West as part of the tradition of what James Ellroy calls American tragic realism, one of the masters of that tradition, with Raymond Chandler and, I might add, James Ellroy. But what is Chandler? English? American-born English? American-born, English-educated writer? American-born, English-educated, American oil business executive, then writer? All of the above and more. One of the people I see in this tradition is Edward Hopper. What is Hopper? A Nyack, New York, painter or a painter of America? What is Whistler? For that matter, what is the master, Henry James? One might say an Atlantic novelist, as we now speak of "Atlantic history."

My point is that the stereotypical presentation of literary realities is not only inaccurate but also not terribly helpful. It does not—for all its revisionist protestations—move us forward. Moreover, it is embarrassingly wrong and unfair. Many of us, for example, were inoculated with the notion that writing in America, far from being a northeast male WASP activity, was, in fact, a *southern* activity. There is something special (we were told) about the South; it produced such writers as Faulkner and Williams, McCullers and Welty, and gave us people such as Willie Morris who *were*, in many cases, the New York literary establishment. Obviously, the southern strategy is also stereotypical, but there is no doubt that it is an extremely common view. To advance the northeast male WASP view and expect automatic agreement overlooks the way in which American literature *was* slanted or "constructed" for many of us.

What has intrigued me about the culture wars is the motivation for making ahistoric assertions and for indulging in combative behavior. Many of those assertions bear little relation to my personal experience. Thus, what I have attempted to do here is look at a number of noteworthy issues that have occasioned combat, reflect on them in light of my reading and personal experience, and lean on Johnson for advice and support in the process. My intention is to contextualize past issues in useful ways and begin to look toward the future.

My own perspective is a somewhat uncommon one, combining as it does such apparently disparate interests as eighteenth-century thought, twentieth-century popular culture, and contemporary genre fiction. I hope that their use in combination is not distracting; I believe that it would trouble Johnson less than it would later critics, and I believe that eclecticism and the convergence of high and popular culture, which some have seen as characteristically postmodern, provides some support for the practice. Like all essays, these are built upon personal experience, but the personal dimension is here more explicit than usual. A Johnsonian framework offers greater latitude for the inclusion of the personal. I have also drawn upon some of my experiences in university administration. Thus, I ask the reader's indulgence as I move between intellectual history, genre fiction, popular culture, educational statistics, and personal reminiscences.

It is not a common combination. Whether or not it is a useful one I leave to the judgment of the reader. Whether my own use of these materials is successful or not is less important to me than my belief that the issues we confront every day can be elucidated by combinations such as these. One of the key themes of the essays is the extent to which contemporary academic commentary on literature is often too pat, too predictable, too imitative, too derivative.

We say that we seek new bodies of material and new approaches to them, but the economy of the profession often vitiates that process. I see a strong parallel between what has recently transpired in the world of letters and what, in Tom Wolfe's view, has transpired in the world of twentieth-century architecture. Academics, fleeing in horror from anything smacking of the bourgeois, offer us something far worse: bland sameness presented in elitist terms in the name of the poor. The alternative practices to which I attempt to point involve, I believe, both a return to the eighteenth century and the practice of its pivotal figure as well as an appropriate posture for the cultural situation in which we presently find ourselves. Johnson is closer to us than we often recognize. One of my intentions is to make that proximity more apparent.

To bridge the gap between the twentieth century and the eighteenth is, at first sight, a significant challenge, though I will later argue that the step is a shorter and easier one than we might at first recognize. The appearance of difficulty arises in part from the fact that our current situation is characterized by a series of significant disjunctions that are omnipresent in our literary and professional experience. I have termed these disjunctions separations. Since the present plight of literary study results in part from certain elements of romanticism, it is altogether appropriate that that plight be characterized by one of romanticism's great themes.

We now regularly experience the separation of poetry from society, of writers from critics, and of theorists from historians, biographers, and editors. Our professional societies are detached from profound issues of national educational policy, elites from the rank and file, academics from the larger reading public. The gulf between our major research universities and the larger world of American education continues to widen, high culture (in key particulars) separates from popular culture, black writing from white, female writing from male, language from meaning, texts from the world.

I see these separations as traceable to a set of phenomena: the rise of middle-class writing in the seventeenth century and its ascendancy in the eighteenth; the counternorms of romanticism and their life and growth within university English departments; and the continuation of an Aristotelian, genre-driven, plot-driven ethos in popular culture that is either scorned by the academy or (often) studied in such a way as to nurse the hurts of coteries of the like-minded.

There are also, of course, a number of discrete economic circumstances that have played a role in the development of this situation. These particular separations have been ably charted in David Lodge's novel *Nice Work*. Lodge demonstrates the parallels between academic practices and such modern phenomena as the movement from a manufacturing to a service economy and the displacement of industries that create products by the piratical and parasitical tendencies of modern bankers and financiers.

Lodge suggests that we need not succumb to the circumstances in which we find ourselves and that, indeed, we might even learn from one another as we bridge gulfs and heal fissures. The enemy of this process (a second important theme in the essays that follow) is the tendency toward either/or absolutism, the tendency to characterize all disputes in stark terms of black or white, a form of characterization that is absurd on its face, belies the rich complexities of art, culture, and humanity, and advances careers through separation, exclusion, and the marking of territory.

Identity politics is its most recent offshoot, a system of behaviors that grotesquely oversimplifies the depth and complexity of human experience, dividing people into groups by specially selected (and systematically excluded) characteristics. Russell Jacoby has recently depicted the dimensions of this complexity and the striking avoidance of obvious fact by some of the cultural warriors in his book *Dogmatic Wisdom: How the Culture Wars Divert Education and Distract America* (1994). In his book *The Twilight of Common Dreams: Why America Is Wracked by Culture Wars* (1995), Todd Gitlin has made an admirable case for communication rather than confrontation and for commonality rather than conflict, an effort we might all applaud.

The essays that follow are an attempt to contribute to that process. I have chosen the essay form because of its attendant tentativeness and modesty. No one has the final answers to the many questions that have become the occasion for battles or skirmishes within the culture wars. It is my hope that the addition of an individual perspective may serve to add further nuance to discussions in which positions have tended to harden and separate.

The book might have been subtitled *Some Postmortem Reflections*. It does not pretend to argue a thesis from point *a* to point *b*. Rather, it attempts to examine separate issues with an eye on common themes. Chapters 1 and 4 focus in particular on the separations between writing and criticism. Chapter 2 looks at the academic world and the separations between it and the external realities surrounding it. Chapter 3 examines the separation of professionalized criticism and theory from history, tradition, and specific cultural realities as well as the separation of texts from readers and writers. Chapter 5 looks at the relationships between art and life and art and society, while chapter 6 looks at the professoriate and society, generational disjunctions, and, again, the separations between criticism and various external realities. The final chapter offers a brief synthesis and summary, suggests a thesis temporarily held in abeyance, and returns to the unique perspective of Johnson, the subject of the opening chapter.

I

JOHNSON: THE WRITER AS CRITIC

One of my overarching premises in the essays that follow is that the split between writing and criticism, which is now characteristic of literary practice, has been detrimental to criticism. Leaving that question in abeyance for the moment, but recognizing that any model to whom I might turn would be an individual capable of bridging that gap, it is still fair to ask, why Johnson? If one were focusing on critics who had also been writers, one could select Sidney, Dryden, Coleridge, Arnold, Eliot, Auden, or any of a number of interesting individuals.

In the first place, Johnson has been singled out as a model on numerous occasions, both by professional writers and by academicians, who have found in his work a pattern or patterns that all, to some degree, might attempt to emulate. Eliot considered Johnson to be (with Dryden and Coleridge) one of the three greatest English critics of poetry (p. 184). Leavis said of him that "he is a classic *qua* critic" ("Johnson as Critic," p. 70). Yvor Winters, noting the rarity of great criticism, commented that "perhaps the only critic in English who deserves that epithet is Samuel Johnson" (p. 240). Henri Peyre, a man sensitive to the many failures of criticism, acknowledged Johnson's preeminence among the English critics (p. 4). More recently, Johnson has received praise of a similar order ("Johnson, the greatest critic in the language") from Harold Bloom (p. 28), who, like the rest of these individuals, does not dispense such praise lightly.

Nineteen years ago, William Bowman Piper published an essay entitled "Samuel Johnson as an Exemplary Critic." Lamenting the growing distance between the contemporary critical community and the world of everyday literary experience, Piper saw a replaying of the eighteenth-century confrontation between abstract, continental rationalism and inductive, British empiricism, a conflict in which the self-sufficiency of the rationalist was contrasted with the authentic human experience of the empiricist. For our own times, this is not an idle parallel. English science and satire divested itself of continental rationalism in the seventeenth century. Swift, for example, condemned Descartes to the fate of being swept away into one of his own, fanciful vortices, an experience that recalls the recent comment of a religious wag that no one now goes to limbo except those who continue to believe in it. Satire aside, however, Descartes's influence has remained remarkably strong in France since the seventeenth century, and the recent and strong French influence on Anglo-American thought has represented a striking alteration in direction, as Helen Gardner has noted. While some contemporary literary rationalists seek to subsume their aesthetic feelings under immutable principles, what Piper calls "cultural critics" attempt "to submit their personal experiences of literature to the discussions and disagreements" of their fellow citizens. Their "primary base of reference," Piper writes, is society, not reason, and "for them the critical exercise is not essentially rational, but essentially cultural" (p. 461). Johnson, in Piper's judgment, is the finest exemplar of this approach.

More recently, in an essay entitled "How Departments Commit Suicide," Hazard Adams comments, "Most contemporary writing, I must admit, irritates me. I wish they could all write like Hume and call a spade a spade like Johnson" (p. 35). In addition to his candor and clarity, there are many aspects of Johnson's critical posture to which we might point; in the next several pages I would like to summarize a number of the more notable facets of Johnson's personal experience and critical orientation. The most striking conclusion that can be drawn from that pattern is the remarkable distance that separates Johnson's practice from our own, particularly in light of the regard in which he continues to be held. In short, while we continue to hold his thought and writings in high regard, we continue to sit quietly by as our own practices increasingly diverge from his.

The most obvious characteristic difference between Johnson and modern practitioners of criticism is that Johnson was a professional writer. Thus, we should continue to think of him as he was—not as a skittish Renaissance nobleman circulating sonnets or romances among his friends while shunning publication; not as a self-dramatizing romantic, writing and rewriting the epic account of his own experience (though there is a good bit of self-portraiture in Johnson); and certainly not as the modern academic poet or art novelist, writing for a small audience or cult readership. No, Johnson was the professional writer par excellence, working in currently popular genres, preparing reference works that met market needs, furnishing headnotes and the force of his name for major editorial projects, ghostwriting, doing payment-per-line journalism, and, in general, participating in a process in which the principal activity of the writer was the exchange of manuscripts for sterling.

Johnson's students—like other contemporary literary commentators—are largely academic writers who write for money only in indirect ways. Johnson's inferred view of this growing tribe is far from laudatory. The ultimate claim to poetical honors, he tells us, must come from "the common sense of readers uncorrupted with literary prejudices" (Brown, p. 124), and he states that "common sense and common honesty" are "names of greater authority than that of *Horace*." He deplores "the cant of those who judge by principles rather than perception" (Brown, p. 105) and we know that in his reading—both in his own works and in the works of others—his response was direct, honest, and personal. As he read, he frequently burst into laughter or tears. The terror and fear he experienced from reading books were neither stylized nor mannered, but authentic responses. As he approached life on a very direct level, so did he approach books. And why not? For Johnson both were closely related. "In questions that relate to the heart of man," he wrote, "the common voice of the multitude uninstructed by precept, and unprejudiced by authority," is "more decisive than the learning of Lipsius" (*Rambler* 52, Yale *Works*, 3:280).

A few years ago a speaker at Georgetown recalled his studies at Williams College in the early 1960s. He commented on the fact that his Shakespeare teacher advised the class to get a good rest over the weekend so that they might prepare themselves for what would be one of the most emotionally wrenching experiences of their young lives, namely their impending reading of *King Lear*. Such advice must now seem quaint in the extreme to contemporary critic-theorists; the spirit of the comment, of course, directly mirrors the response of Johnson.

A frequently heard remark, that academic battles are so fierce because the stakes are so small, is often attributed to Henry Kissinger, but Johnson commented on these matters two centuries earlier:

> It is not easy to discover from what cause the acrimony of a scholiast can naturally proceed. The subjects to be discussed by him are of very small importance; they involve neither property nor liberty; nor favour the interest of sect or party. . . . But, whether it be that "small things make mean men proud," and vanity catches small occasions; or that all contrariety of opinion, even in those that can defend it no longer, makes proud men angry; there is often found in commentaries a spontaneous strain of invective and contempt, more eager and venomous than is vented by the most furious controvertist in politicks against those whom he is hired to defame. ("Preface to Shakespeare," Yale *Works*, 7:102)

Johnson's interest in literature was far from academic, and it was not, ultimately, aesthetic. He recognized art and praised it, but he went to books to learn of men and of life. Like Aristotle, Horace, and Sidney, he knew that poetry must be done well because its production did not meet an absolute human need. His own interest was in what we would call the psychological or, purged of unfavorable associations, the behavioral. He was fascinated by the things that human beings do and the reasons why they do them, a fascination that, for him, could be expressed in religious and moral terms as well as in psychological ones.

To be a Johnsonian critic is, thus, to see literature as a part of the totality of human experience and to resist the temptations of narrow focus and narrow specialization. To adopt a Johnsonian posture would mean nothing less than the de-professionalization of literary study as we know it, for one cannot follow Johnson into all of the realms of his interests (military history, for example, chemistry, medicine, law, theology, linguistics, and numismatics) and continue to be able to devote all of one's waking hours to the unending pursuit of a single, narrowly defined subject. Joseph Wood Krutch, among others, has misleadingly described Johnson's reading as "casual" and "unsystematic" (pp. 12, 87, 287–88), seeing it in many ways as a curious feature or behavior rather than as a central way of proceeding. The rich breadth of Johnson's reading *is* the system.

Johnson's tastes were broad, his interest in all aspects of human experience, including popular culture, strong. When we think of him in London we should think of him at public shows, not at concerts or at the theatre, where he was often uncomfortable or bored. We should think of him being fascinated with the newest automata or observing balloon ascents, going to Bedlam, or observing such displays as the performances of the famous learned pig. We know that he liked museums filled with curiosities and popular public resorts such as Ranelagh. He was interested in the workings of machinery and, living at the beginning of the industrial revolution, was able to grasp the mechanical principles involved in contemporary inventions with uncommon acuity.

His literary reading was not confined to highbrow texts. We know, for example, that he was an avid reader of romances. In fact, the comparative absence of those books that we know he enjoyed from the sale catalogue of his library should serve as a warning to us that we not use that document uncritically. It may be that the commonness of many of his possessions made them less attractive at auction and they now exist as part of numbered lots rather than as specified titles.

Johnson wrote to the student Strahan advising him to not omit mingling "some lighter books with those of more importance; that which is read *remisso animo* is often of great use, and takes great hold of the remembrance" (*The Letters of Samuel Johnson*, 1:248). We know that he certainly did this himself and that many lighter books not only provided him pleasure but also enriched his understanding of human behavior. Note that Johnson is a great defender of pleasure per se, whose decline in our own times Lionel Trilling once lamented. Both in his actions and in his reading, it is clear that Johnson combines a deft discipline with a healthy sense of whimsy, so that his scholarly work always carries with it an imaginative dimension that enlivens and enriches, just as his approach to common life and common culture carries with it a combination of thoughtfulness and incisiveness that is equally rare.

As a professional writer, Johnson's critical judgment is often focused upon craft. The manner in which his thought is expressed has more in common with modern how-to books (Scott Meredith's guide to novel writing or Syd Field's advice on screenwriting, for example) than with academic criticism:

> Whatever professes to benefit by pleasing must please at once. The pleasures of the mind imply something sudden and unexpected; that which elevates must always surprise. What is perceived by slow de-

grees may gratify us with the consciousness of improvement, but will never strike with the sense of pleasure. (Brown, p. 66)

[Shakespeare accomplishes] the *first* purpose of a writer, by exciting . . . him that reads his work to read it through. ("Preface to Shakespeare," Yale *Works*, 7:83)

To a thousand cavils one answer is sufficient; the purpose of a writer is to be read, and the criticism which would destroy the power of pleasing must be blown aside. (*Life of Pope, Lives of the English Poets*, 3:240)

Prior to the nineteenth century, as R. S. Crane argued many years ago ("English Neoclassical Criticism: An Outline Sketch," pp. 375-76), criticism was more often rhetorical than philosophical. The traditions that Johnson associated with such figures as Horace and Quintilian or, later, Vida and Vossius are as foreign to much modern experience as they were useful to practicing writers. How many contemporary critics and theorists would look at something like Bysshe's *Art of English Poetry* (1702), an extremely popular text, manual, and guide of its time, with rules for making verses, collections of singular passages, and a rhyming dictionary? Scolar reproduced it in facsimile twenty years ago; who would do so today? Yet Johnson used Bysshe, just as he used John Walker's more comprehensive rhyming dictionary (1775). Walker's *Elements of Elocution* (1781) was in fact dedicated to Johnson.

Such materials are guides for professional writers, not for academic critics, who would largely ridicule contemporary equivalents, materials prepared by practitioners, which is to say, professionals, but that only indicates the separation in our own lives between the discussion of literature and the writing of literature. Academic professionalism is expected; the professionalism of the writer is suspect.

For Johnson the relationship between art and life is far closer than it is for us. Similarly, the processes that produce art and the responses that art evokes are also matters that command his close attention. The nearly complete lack of interest in the creative process and the frequent separation of the artist from the common reader as well as from society are points to which I will later return. Here I would note the radical difference between Johnson's ethos and our own. The period of his life, 1709 to 1784, is not only pre-romantic but, perhaps equally important, pre-academic. The only truly noteworthy writer with a strong academic connection in Johnson's time was Thomas Gray, a poet whose output was notably sparse, a writer with a cult following (including Boswell), some of whose most popular work Johnson critically eviscerated. Adam Smith was also an academic, but one, it should be noted, who was not narrowly specialized. Smith wrote on economics, of course, but he lectured on philosophy and rhetoric as well; Boswell was one of his students.

The eighteenth-century model—of which Johnson is a great exemplar—is, in general, decidedly nonacademic. Readers of Boswell will remember Johnson's visit to Oxford in 1754 in which he calls on his fellow collegian, the Reverend John Meeke (*Boswell's Life of Johnson*, 1:272–74). Johnson recalls Meeke's intimidating academic prowess in his youth, a superiority that has evaporated as he has remained within the academic groves.

> About the same time of life, Meeke was left behind at Oxford to feed on a Fellowship, and I went to London to get my living: now, Sir, see the difference of our literary characters! (p. 274)

The anecdote is perfect, even down to poor Meeke's real-life tag name. The account comes from Thomas Warton, who, four years later, would include a "Journal of a Senior Fellow" in *Idler* 33. The following are representative entries (all from Johnson, Yale *Works*, 2:103):

> Returned to my room. Made a tiff of warm punch, and to bed before nine; did not fall asleep till ten, a young fellow-commoner being very noisy over my head. . . .
> At dinner in the hall. Too much water in the soup. Dr. Dry always orders the beef to be salted too much for me. . . .
> Returned home, and stirred my fire. Went to the common-room, and supped on the snipes with Dr. Dry.

And so on. One can nearly feel the gray matter turning to pudding.

One of the obvious reasons for this pattern of nonacademic literary activity was the paucity of academic posts; careers had to be sought elsewhere, for example, in medicine (Locke, Arbuthnot, Blackmore, Goldsmith, and Smollett), the law (Boswell and, later, Scott), and in the church (Bishops Sprat, Berkeley, and Percy; Swift, Sterne, Young, Blair, and Crabbe, who also practiced medicine). Defoe and Richardson were businessmen; among Defoe's many works are important materials on trade. In a modern university he might well be more comfortable in a school of business than in a department of English. In the imaginary college in St. Andrews that Johnson and Boswell fantasized over, Johnson was to teach theology, not literary criticism (or literary theory). However, considering Percy's position as a clergyman, Johnson agreed to cede practical divinity to his friend; Johnson himself would teach logic, metaphysics, and scholastic divinity (*Boswell's Journal of A Tour to the Hebrides with Samuel Johnson, L.L.D.*, pp. 78–79).

Even more important, the majority of eighteenth-century writers and thinkers were far more involved in the actions of their societies than are their modern North American counterparts. Jonathan Swift, who successfully defended the Irish from the minting of debased copper coinage, was in part opposing Isaac Newton, who, in addition to his scientific and theological research, was serving as Master of the Mint.

Matthew Prior, the poet, had served as secretary to the ambassador at The Hague and was employed in the negotiations for the Treaty of Ryswick. Later, Prior participated in the negotiations for the Treaty of Utrecht, sometimes called "Matt's Peace." David Hume accompanied Lieutenant General James St. Clair as judge-advocate in the expedition to Lorient in 1747 and on a mission to Vienna and Turin in 1748. He also served as undersecretary of state, as did Prior, Joseph Addison, Thomas Tickell, Nicholas Rowe, and Richard Brinsley Sheridan.

Boswell not only supported the Corsicans in their struggle for independence with his pen but also raised sufficient funds to purchase £700 worth of ordnance for them, which was shipped to Leghorn in 1768 (£700 equaling approximately £30,000 in modern currency).

Defoe (like Chaucer and probably Marlowe) was employed as a governmental secret agent, working in Scotland in support of the Union. Henry Fielding, the novelist, playwright, journalist, and satirist, was justice of the peace for Westminster. Lord Kames, author of *The Elements of Criticism*, was, like Monboddo the pioneer anthropologist, a Scottish judge. Gibbon served in the Hampshire militia and (like Andrew Marvell before him) in Parliament. He wrote an extended essay on the study of literature in addition to his classic *Decline and Fall*. Similarly, Edmund Burke, the orator, politician, and political commentator, was the author of an extremely important treatise on aesthetics. While Johnson himself remained a professional writer after his early experimentation with schoolmastering, he wrote numerous political pieces, including volumes of parliamentary debates for the *Gentleman's Magazine*. His published comments on the eighteenth-century conflict over the Falkland Islands were rediscovered by the general public during the most recent conflict there. His work received prominent contemporary attention, in, for example, the *New York Times*.

My intention is not to attempt to idealize the eighteenth century by imagining a society that was more coherent than it actually was. It was often not coherent. However, writers *did* participate in it in public ways, across—it should be noted—the full political spectrum. That was the norm and not the exception, but while Vaclav Havel has taken on the responsibilities of government within the Czech Republic and Mario Vargas Llosa has stood for election in Peru, the North American scene remains remarkably academic and withdrawn. The notion of sending a William Styron, a John Barth, or a Thomas Pynchon to negotiate a major treaty or to stand for election as governor of a state is, here and now, simply unthinkable. It was not always so, and Johnson's approach to literary criticism and scholarship should be seen against the backdrop of a society that integrated thought, art, and action to a far greater degree than our own. Similarly, the eighteenth century was able to produce individuals who were fully capable of writing serious history, economics, or political commentary along with literary criticism and literary theory.

Johnson's own practice is built upon a very small theoretical superstructure, most of which William R. Keast outlined many years ago. Essentially, Johnson demands two things of art: novelty and truth, truth understood to mean faithfulness to the observations and conclusions of human psychology. If the artifact repeats received truth in a predictable fashion, it is like a message from a fortune cookie. If it is only new and not, as Johnson is wont to say, true or just, it is merely an oddity. It must be both novel *and* true. It must do just things in fresh ways. Essentially, this is a prescription for successful work within established genres, and as a norm it is very much alive and well in those areas of our culture that continue to specialize in genre-driven narrative: principally cinema and television programming. Johnson's demands of art are precisely those of the stereotypical script reader, studio chief, or production company executive, as in Robert Altman's film *The Player* or Elmore Leonard's novel *Get Shorty*. Bring me something that is new that is also tried and true.

In the Jenyns review Johnson articulates his famous principle that writing should enable the reader to better enjoy life or better endure it (Schwartz, *Samuel Johnson and the Problem of Evil*, p. 108), a strongly pragmatic judgment that highlights his respect for writing (or any other form of human activity) that entertains us harmlessly, harmless pleasure being that which is at least morally neutral and which has no attending bad consequences. He says of the Scriblerus *Memoirs* that "it has been little read, or when read has been forgotten, as no man could be wiser, better, or merrier, by remembering it" (*Life of Pope, Lives*, 3:182). This is a notion that should receive greater attention in still-puritan America, where we often distinguish genres on the basis of levels of perceived seriousness (for example, "escapist" fiction), assuming that there is something inherently suspicious in pleasure that necessitates our giving lower marks to those who provide it. This is a culturally constructed view. The French (many of whose other theories we have recently come to embrace), for example, have far greater regard for this dimension of popular culture than we do, because popular culture is interesting and instructive as well as, often, amusing. Barthes, after all, studied such things as professional wrestling and automobile design. How many "serious" academics would have dared do such a thing at that time in America besides Leslie Fiedler?

Johnson's understanding of art is based on wide experience of it, and his judgments are largely comparative—examining endless examples of similar texts to determine what is just and what is novel. The purpose is not to make absolutist value judgments, though Johnson is capable of such judgments, but rather to draw subtle distinctions concerning individual texts by calling upon wide experience of the multiplicity of variations and permutations that mark other examples within the category under scrutiny.

This is coupled with his interest in human psychology. Johnson, like the late Kenneth Burke, is deeply interested in what Burke called "literature as equipment for living," and this broad conception of the function of literature, combined with his interest in popular culture, results in a set of intellectual behaviors that involve both the identification of distinguished texts and the simultaneous desire to continue to broaden the canon, to search for new writers, new forms, new embodiments of wisdom, and new techniques. It would be Johnsonian practice to identify texts that excel in certain respects by comparing them with texts similar in kind (that is, with common themes, settings, subject matter, or technique). This would particularly apply to the identification of texts that, in Burke's terms, add words to an informal dictionary that clarifies and depicts human behavior by providing the "strategic naming of a situation," for example, "Bovarysme" (Adams, *Critical Theory since Plato*, p. 945).

The Burke/Johnson parallel is a nice one for another reason. As Frank Lentricchia has argued, Burke sets himself against the

> aestheticist doctrine at the heart of modernist theory: Art is not a kind of distinctive substance...but, rather, a type of oppositional activity in the world, a discordant and disruptive voice out to "undermine any one rigid scheme of living." (*Criticism and Social Change*, pp. 88–89)

For Burke, as for Johnson, art plays a role within a society; it does not drift away into the attractive but withdrawn space putatively constructed by the Kant of the *Critique of Judgment*. Moreover, it is not seen, simplemindedly, as a dominance tool. Most serious writing is countercultural, although—Johnson would argue—it should not all be so. We require a culture as well as a counterculture. (Interestingly, the most obvious defenders of art's role in reinforcing culture and government have probably been the Platonic Socrates of books 2 and 3 of the *Republic* and such modern totalitarians as the German National Socialists and Soviet Communists.)

The desire to expand our literary and cultural horizons is one of the norms of contemporary literary study, but it is arguable that Johnson's approach is far more likely to be effective in achieving that end than the more academic approaches and preoccupations that we most frequently encounter. Forays into the vast territories of category fiction or nonfiction prose, for example, are likely to yield a broader field of inquiry than the narrowing of critical activity to the subjection of candidate texts to theoretical tests, particularly monolithic or, indeed, ideological tests.

Johnson's qualifications as a commentator on literature are, increasingly, different from those expected of many modern critic/scholars. There are three areas in particular where his preparation was, in many respects, unparalleled: the knowledge of texts, the knowledge of language, and the knowledge of books as physical objects.

Johnson's father, of course, was a bookseller, and his son was exposed early to an array of books that, for his time, was sizeable. There were no lending libraries as we know them until the nineteenth century, and private collections often remained just that—private. Johnson could call upon the rich resources of his father's shop for reading, for browsing, and for schoolbooks; we know, for example, the titles of the approximately 115 volumes that Johnson took along to Oxford (Reade, *Johnsonian Gleanings*, 5:28).

Johnson was exposed not only to books but also to the book trade. In addition to his Lichfield location and the setting up of stalls in provincial markets, Michael Johnson was also involved for a time in a binding operation, and his son later was able to impress his friends with his knowledge of the binder's craft. The binding business would, of course, have involved the obtaining of hides, and it is possible that Johnson traveled with his father on his jaunts to secure them.

In the early 1740s, Johnson was involved in the cataloguing of the great private library of Robert Harley, the earl of Oxford. Upon the death of the second earl, Harley's son, the bookseller Osborne purchased the collection (a £13,000 risk) and paid for the compilation of the catalogue to promote its sale. Working with William Oldys, Johnson was hired to produce the massive four-volume catalogue of the library and personally edit the *Harleian Miscellany*, an eight-volume selection of rare political and religious pamphlets contained within the collection. These were exhaustive undertakings, with literally thousands of publications passing through Johnson's hands.

Johnson's next major project was nothing less than the production of a dictionary of the English language—an enormous two-folio-volume edition with thousands upon thousands of illustrative quotations supporting the definitions: a seven-year project accomplished with the assistance of six amanuenses. Modern users of the dictionary should keep in mind what Johnson was fond of keeping in mind, namely that it had taken forty members of the French Academy forty years to complete their dictionary. While the French operated with government support, Johnson worked with a syndicate of private publishers who had advanced the fifteen hundred guineas required for the project.

As if that were not enough, Johnson next edited the works of William Shakespeare, utilizing his massive knowledge of Elizabethan English and plunging himself into the multiplicity of textual problems that every Shakespearian editor is forced to confront. Later in his life he took on the task of writing biographical/critical prefaces (some over a hundred pages in length) to the works of fifty-two English poets, this in addition to his own poetic work, essays, fiction, travel writing, reviews, parliamentary debates, political commentary, sermons, co-authored law lectures, diaries, prayers, prefaces, dedications, fugitive pieces, letters, and biographies.

First and foremost, as I have indicated, he knew books. He knew books as a binder, a bookseller, a librarian, a collector, and a cataloguer knows books. He knew language, and he knew it as a philologist and as (only) a lexicographer does. And he knew texts as an editor must know them. He knew texts as a commentator must know them. He knew texts as a bibliographer must know them. The fact that he could combine such specialized, technical knowledge with the skills and concerns of the professional writer and the instincts and responses of the amateur reader, that is, the individual who does what he does out of love and personal interest, helps to make Johnson the remarkable and incomparable commentator on literature that he is.

But which of these experiences do we now see as essential for the modern critic/scholar? We do require a knowledge of books, but I would argue that the tendencies of academic criticism narrow their number rather than expand them. We require some knowledge of language, but we appear to be more comfortable with the knowledge of discrete *theories* of language (sometimes knowledge of *a* theory of language) than with the expectation of extensive knowledge of language itself. (That theory, Saussure's, for example, might also be one that modern linguists would see as important but dated.) And textual bibliography? That is practiced by relatively few and required of relatively few. An individual like Jerome McGann who moves between theory, historiography, and editorial concerns is extremely rare. An individual like Leslie Fiedler, trained philologically but comfortable with the materials of popular culture, is equally rare. Lexicographers prepared to take on gargantuan projects—like Frederic Cassidy, still hard at work on his *Dictionary of American Regional English*—are now virtually nonexistent. Academic critics who produce (or produced) serious fiction, verse, or nonfiction prose have been rare, though we can point to individuals such as Tate, Trilling, Ransom, Winters, Josephine Miles, Anthony Hecht, John Hollander, and Norman Maclean. In America, public intellectuals such as Edmund Wilson have largely disappeared, and many writers who have done semischolarly work for a wide audience, such as Isaac Asimov, are not taken very seriously by their academic counterparts (though Asimov did hold an academic post in chemistry for many years).

To imagine Johnson today, we would have to piece together the abilities and experiences of a half-dozen or dozen individuals, for the activities and traditions that he personally conducted and embodied are now dispersed and displaced, often, unfortunately, under the pressures of academic criticism. At a minimum, one might think of his modern counterpart as a combination of Fiedler (the interest in human psychology, popular culture, and literature as the reflection of life within a society), Asimov (in productivity and the size of tasks undertaken), Wilson (in the breadth of his interests and nonacademic posture), Sir James Murray (as lexicographer), Eliot or Winters (as a practicing poet *and* critic), Pound (as an encourager of others, like Coleridge), and perhaps Churchill, not in his American blood, of course, but rather in his personal curiosities, his Englishness, his prolific writing, his wit, his awesome verbal agility, his great courage, and his estimable resilience in dealing with political opponents, military enemies, and personal demons.

Schopenhauer once compared the true critic with the phoenix; one appears only every five hundred years. The point of the Johnson example is not to continually remind us of how far short we fall of the ideal (or an ideal). Rather, it is to take an individual whose work has long commanded respect, to see what aspects of that work are supported by (or diminished by) current academic practices, and to use that work to help orient us as we move beyond the culture wars to new practices in the study of literature. I will argue that there is a possible convergence of emerging inclination with established Johnsonian practice. A Johnsonian perspective on the culture wars themselves, even what will often be an imagined or reconstructed perspective, can serve to elucidate them, to separate the smoke from the light and the originals from the mirrors and to aid us in clarifying our present position. At the same time, it can help us look beyond to the kinds of activities that might fruitfully engage our attention and enlist our energies in the coming decades.

However one feels about Johnson's critical orientation (there is, for example, strong opposition from many camps to anything that smacks of the judicial or the mimetic), it must be admitted that he is often right and never dull. We should remember that many theorists do not listen to or learn from one another; many—in their inconsistencies—seem not to be listening to themselves. Artists do not generally follow the theorists' theories, at least not in any consistent ways. Thus, we have a great deal of Blakean theorizing, that is, individuals constructing their own systems so that they will not be enslaved by those of others, and many instances of the adoption of facets of theoretical approaches by followers grasping for handles on currently prominent, moving bandwagons. There is nothing inherently wrong with that, so long as we realize that the theories articulated are not generally expected to consistently apply to practice. They may help to interpret some past or specific practice, but few are ever expected to apply to all practice. What *is* imitated is technique. What *is* utilized is a vocabulary. That is different, however, from the systematic verification of a theory. My point is that if Johnson has been labeled unsystematic, much of what is considered to be rigorously systematic is less so than is claimed.

Those theorists whose work is designed to apply to all literature are actually few in number. Frye is the most prominent example, and while Frye has been extremely influential, he is more influential in the details of his writing (or in the courage of his endeavor) than in his theory per se.

There is a strong parallel here with Johnson. Frye too is never dull. He is always instructive. There is an insight or two on practically every page that he has written, around which someone somewhere might build a doctoral dissertation. Like Johnson and other estimable minds with whom one will often disagree (C. S. Lewis, for example), the greatness is often in little things: passages, terms, heuristic devices, techniques. Large theories come and go; few (Aristotle's, for example) remain. What does remain are hints, principles, phrases, and formulations, guideposts that teach us how to read. Here Johnson is supreme, in great part because of the nature of the experience—both personal and literary—that he is capable of bringing to bear.

2

CANONS AND CULTURE WARS

The recurring images are by now familiar ones: in the nightmares of the right, Stanford students gleefully celebrate the revision of their undergraduate curriculum and the attendant devaluation of the white, phallologocentric, western tradition. The sound track is a deafening hum of mantra-like chants; in the background can be seen the smoke and flames from a large bonfire. The cultural death grip has finally been broken.

In the nightmares of the left, Secretary of Education William Bennett appears on an ersatz mountain of canonical texts wielding a bullhorn, expressing his opinions of Stanford's curricular initiatives. The penitent faculty put on hairshirts, bow respectfully before the secretary, and promptly overturn the revisions. The students toast the decision with Savory and James Amontillado, don tweed jackets and white gloves, and repair to the library to read their Livy.

It is useful to have events that help to focus discussions and debates. Blake speaks repeatedly of the importance of what he terms *contraries* and how the friction generated by opposition can lead to truth, a pattern Johnson observed and charted in the practices of the metaphysical poets. The ultimate importance of symbolic events must, however, also be assessed.

Clifford Adelman, a researcher for the Department of Education, has done extensive studies of student academic behavior, principally, but not exclusively, enrollment decisions. He wisely studies transcripts—in the tens of thousands—rather than decanal pronouncements or college catalogues and bulletins, many of which fail to adequately reflect academic realities. His interest, in short, is the manner in which students—within the constraints of their institutional systems—vote with their feet, not the manner in which a curriculum is formally described or puffed. In Adelman's considered judgment, the revision of the Stanford curriculum—while an interesting phenomenon—is an episode of very little importance in the larger scheme of things. That larger scheme, of course, is a system of higher education in the United States of America in which precious few institutions share the opportunities or, indeed, bear even the slightest resemblance to Stanford University.

The *Chronicle of Higher Education*'s 1993 almanac identifies 3,601 institutions of higher education in the United States and 6,382 vocational institutions. Very few of the former and virtually none of the latter have much in common with the institution that is Leland Stanford's legacy. Many of our fellow citizens enrolled in community colleges, beauticians' schools, and colleges of applied science may not even have heard of Stanford University, and debates concerning multiculturalism and the western tradition doubtless seem quite remote in their classrooms, where a truly multicultural group of individuals is struggling desperately to develop marketable skills in a difficult economy. Thus, to focus upon such matters as canons and canonicity, the culture wars, and the importance (or oppressiveness) of the western tradition is to choose, as defining phenomena, phenomena that are of relatively small importance in American education, broadly considered.

Such a utilitarian judgment is open to criticism of various sorts, though it has been argued expertly by Russell Jacoby in his most recent book, *Dogmatic Wisdom*. For example, it is true that while the cultural wars rage on comparatively few battlefields, those battlefields are the campuses upon which a disproportionate share of the nation's intellectual, industrial, and governmental leaders are educated and trained. Many of these institutions are major research universities, and their faculty produce the scholarship and the textbook material whose effects ripple through the rest of American higher education. What happens at Stanford—from a certain perspective—is more important culturally and historically than what happens at hundreds of other institutions combined.

Nevertheless, Adelman has a point. We should be more concerned, for example, at the fact that a large proportion of American undergraduates are really enrolled in professional schools, principally schools of business, education, and engineering. They are being trained, but are they being educated? The situation at the graduate level is equally instructive. In 1990-91 there were 1,416 doctoral degrees awarded in letters, but 2,640 professional degrees in chiropractic, 1,115 in optometry, 1,459 in osteopathic medicine, 1,244 in pharmacy, and 2,032 in veterinary medicine. There were 5,695 theological degrees awarded, 15,043 M.D. degrees awarded, and a whopping—but not surprising—37,945 law degrees. (The issue of "multicultural" versus "western" education pales somewhat when we consider the number of students seeking professional rather than liberal education and when we consider the size of those fields surrounding the battlefields on which the cultural wars are fought.) We should be more concerned—with Adelman—at the fact that a large proportion of undergraduates seldom move beyond introductory coursework in fields outside of their majors. We should be more concerned at the fact that a large proportion of undergraduates remain ignorant of higher mathematics and foreign languages. In short, we should be more concerned about the general state of higher *education* as it is experienced by *all* of our fellow citizens who are enrolled in its institutions.

As educators we should be more aware than we usually are of the place of proprietary schools in American education. Both as taxpayers and fellow human beings, we should be knowledgeable about the access these institutions have to such resources as federal loan monies and the extent to which they offer needed economic opportunity (or, in some cases, fail to offer needed economic opportunity) to their graduates. These institutions take one of every five federal loan dollars, and the default rate on those loans is approximately 35 percent. Johnson measures societies by their willingness and ability to make a decent provision for their poor. How much of our teaching and how many of our tax dollars devoted to education are aiding in that process?

There is a great deal of talk within the academy about the extent to which our activities are politicized (necessarily politicized, many would say), but there is very little talk about the actual political realities of American higher education. An event such as the Stanford curriculum revision appears to many to be a high political moment, but that response reflects a distressingly narrow conception of political reality. It may be prime material for Modern Language Association, National Endowment for the Humanities, and Office of Education bully pulpits, but the number of active listeners within those speakers' congregations is comparatively small and the majority of the firm believers are highly unlikely to undergo a conversion experience as a result of an opposition sermon.

I am not attempting to minimize the importance of cultural debates nor the importance of curricula at leading educational institutions. What I am saying is that these matters are a small part of a far larger enterprise and that that larger enterprise should concern the academic participants in the cultural debates far more than it has.

These debates fall within a number of contexts that can serve, I believe, to place them in perspective. I will look at several of these contexts in an attempt to point out that the assumed realities of the debates themselves need to be reconsidered. Essentially, I will argue the following: (1) that virtually no one—speaking in statistical terms—now "possesses" the traditional literary canon as a personal, intellectual resource; (2) that the "traditional" canon does not embody a coherent and consistent system of values that should be rigorously sustained *or* militantly challenged; (3) that arguments for "opening up" the canon (which is assumed to exist in human minds and hearts as well as on paper in books) generally fail to take into account the realities of writing, reading, publishing, and teaching in twentieth-century America; and (4) that while literary academics have pressed for the preservation, revision, or even jettisoning of the traditional canon, the economies that impinge on their profession necessitate a pattern of reading behavior that is usually narrower than that in the larger society of which they are a part.

The positioning of the canon debate is a slippery activity, particularly if one assumes that changes in the canon reflect—as well as determine—cultural change. To some of my colleagues, the modern period begins in the fourth century B.C.; to others it is the period of Joyce, Eliot, and Yeats. My own view is that the modern world begins in the seventeenth century. It is also in the seventeenth century that a number of the principal debates occur with regard to the shape of education and, hence, the formulation of possible new curricula and canons. The chief event is usually described in academic shorthand as the Ancients-Moderns controversy, a succession of events whose English episodes principally touch Swift, one of whose created narrators chronicles an actual battle of the books.

That battle, as conceived by Swift and the Scriblerians, was often more cultural than intellectual. It did not so much concern what books would be read and taught and what cultural artifacts would be preserved as it did a clash between high culture and mass culture—the outrage of the elite at the sudden appearance of the parvenu, the fear that a few great books would be drowned in an ocean of middle-class ink. The apogee of that concern is Pope's *Dunciad*, where the writings of contemporary hacks and poetasters move Pope to feelings that are literally apocalyptic.

In his *Life of Swift*, Johnson scores the Scriblerians for this posture:

> From the letters that pass between him [Swift] and Pope it might be inferred that they, with Arbuthnot and Gay, had engrossed all the understanding and virtue of mankind, that their merits filled the world; or that there was no hope of more. They shew the age involved in darkness, and shade the picture with sullen emulation. (*Lives*, 3:61–62)

Johnson was, of course, aware that mass culture might dilute or in some cases displace high culture, but he also knew that its growth was inevitable. He also found it interesting, both in itself and as an aid to understanding human behavior. He relished popular romances, as I have already noted, and he took a special interest in works whose impact was broad (John Pomfret's poem "The Choice," for example) because that impact and resonance of the works were in and of themselves of interest. In our own time he would, presumably, read writers such as John Grisham and Stephen King to find out what the fuss is about and to determine what psychological and cultural conclusions (if any) could be drawn from the level of acceptance of particular writers and particular works.

Johnson had a rich and realistic sense of human culture and knew that it could no more be fixed and controlled by Scriblerian arbiters meeting at Kensington Palace than the English language could be set and fixed by the members of an English academy. Moreover, he had less taste for the establishment of such a body, indeed, less taste for the company of the rich and powerful than did the Scriblerians. Johnson's clubs met in taverns.

Johnson's own sympathies were not with the ancients (and their Scriblerian defenders) but with the moderns and what Richard Popkin has termed the "constructive skepticism" of the new science of the Renaissance. That science had challenged the authority of the church and the aristocracy and offered new knowledge in place of superstition, indefensible dogma, and authority grounded only in tradition. Pope and Swift, on the other hand, are noticeably reactionary in this regard, and their suspicions of science—like their suspicions of mass culture—essentially ally them with the past.

Among Johnson's many great strengths is his ability to balance his religious and moral beliefs with his respect for the new science. He does this with a deep sense of the human realities in which any new technological developments would be embedded. In other words, while he expected and praised technological advances as a result of the new science, he did not expect changes in human nature to come as rapidly as changes in medicine or machinery. It is Johnson—himself fascinated by the future possibility of heavier-than-air flight as well as by contemporary balloon ascents—who asks, in chapter 6 of *Rasselas*, "What would be the security of the good, if the bad could at pleasure invade them from the sky?," a question that has captioned photographs of the Gough Square residence's attic (in which Johnson's Dictionary was produced) after it was destroyed two centuries later by Nazi bombs in the Battle of Britain.

Johnson neither swings to the secular, utopian extremes of the overly optimistic French, who would live to see Condorcet hunted down by Robespierre and Lavoisier go to the scaffold, nor to the reactionary extremes of the Tory satirists, the last pre-Renaissance men. In short, he is able to embrace the skepticism of the Enlightenment without adopting the radical moral and political postures that so often accompanied it. He is also capable of embracing "traditional" thought and writing within the wider context of human culture, broadly conceived. He knew—to put it in modern terms—that it was both inevitable and desirable that we move beyond the traditional canon.

I will return to this latter point. Here I would like to linger a moment on Johnson's skepticism, a stance he shares with the other towering intellectual figure of eighteenth-century Britain, David Hume. To be sure, Hume lacks Johnson's religious faith, but his rhetoric is imbued with a reverence that is the result of both tolerance and good manners. His posture is never antinomian.

Hume's skepticism is grounded in science and logic, but it is often expressed in much the same fashion as Johnson's, Johnson sharing what the philosophers term Hume's "naturalism." The point was made by Popkin over forty years ago, but it is worth a fresh look, particularly in light of the varieties of academic skepticism one encounters in contemporary cultural debates.

Popkin writes of Hume's "Pyrrhonism and His Critique of Pyrrhonism." While Hume was anxious to demonstrate that there is no *certain* basis for such fundamental beliefs as our trust that the sun will rise in the morning, Hume was equally anxious to demonstrate that irrational beliefs are not subject to rational critique. (This should be compared with Stanley Fish's identification of a characteristic error of the left, namely the mistake of believing that once one has shown that convictions come from culture and not from God, those convictions will automatically be rendered less compelling.) Matters of faith, in short, are off-limits for rationalist philosophers. Having removed certainty from our world—and having done it in wholesale fashion—Hume promptly turns around and notes that this is all quite irrelevant to much of what we term real life.

The claims of nature, Hume argues, are always far more powerful than the claims of reason. Hence, when we are hungry or in need of sleep, we do not engage in skeptical debates about the existence of food or couches. We eat and sleep. The place where this kind of debate *does* flourish, Hume says, is in the academy, and his portrayal of the academician is of an individual living in a private world from which he must be awakened by amused observers. This represents a reversal of the Platonic myth; here, everyone else has been outside in the sunlight while the academic has remained within the cave. (It should also be noted, of course, that there were far fewer academies and academicians in Hume's time than in our own.)

Without belaboring the point here, I would say that there are Humean (and Johnsonian) answers to many of the excesses of contemporary (academic) literary theory. Johnson's application of the commonsense cudgel, for example, is itself often an embodiment of Hume's so-called naturalism, the realization that while one might argue a point of view within the shades of academic groves (an image Hume uses), it dissolves immediately when one walks into the sunlight of reality. Cognitive atheists (E. D. Hirsch's term), for example, who argue that language does not find any clear referent in the outside world, alter their principles instantly when they are reading the prices on a wine list; similarly, those who pose as thoroughgoing relativists are quick to adjust their intellectual stance when faced with the requirement to advise their library's bibliographers concerning the purchase of monographs and serials within the constraints of dwindling budgets.

Hume can speak for himself:

> These [skeptical] principles may flourish and triumph in the schools, where it is indeed difficult, if not impossible, to refute them. But as soon as they leave the shade, and by the presence of the real objects which actuate our passions and sentiments are put in opposition to the more powerful principles of our nature, they vanish like smoke and leave the most determined skeptic in the same condition as other mortals.
>
> And though a *Pyrrhonian* may throw himself or others into a momentary amazement and confusion by his profound reasonings, the first and most trivial event in life will put to flight all his doubts and scruples, and leave him the same, in every point of action and speculation, with the philosophers of every other sect or with those who never concerned themselves in any philosophical researches. (*An Inquiry Concerning Human Understanding*, pp. 167, 168)

My point, in brief, is that by following a Johnsonian model it is possible to challenge established authority and embrace the skepticism that animates and lies at the root of the cultural wars without simultaneously jettisoning the past or taking leave of common sense, just as it is possible to express, simultaneously, a respect for the so-called canon with both the need and the very real desire to move beyond it. I will return to these points throughout the following discussion. Here I wish to reinforce the fact that the cultural wars need not evoke monolithic responses, that, indeed, broader and more generous responses to several key contemporary issues may be found in the eighteenth century, the period that worked through the challenges of skepticism, revolutionary cultural ferment, and unprecedented cultural expansion long before we did.

The book that was chiefly responsible for focusing the modern debate was E. D. Hirsch's *Cultural Literacy: What Every American Needs to Know* (1987). Hirsch, a knowledgeable student of Blake and of continental critical thought, was bestirred to action by his personal education in the area of composition instruction. Having authored a formalistic book (*The Philosophy of Composition*, 1977), Hirsch came to realize that skill-based approaches to reading and writing were inadequate and that students would read and write more effectively if they began their task with some prior familiarity with the subject with which they had to deal.

Hirsch was especially taken with the work of Richard C. Anderson, a specialist in the field of reading at the University of Illinois. He seized upon a particular experiment of Anderson's in which students of different cultures were given texts to read that described weddings within and beyond their own cultures. The texts were comparable in length and complexity and the readers were comparably grouped by age, sex, educational level, marital status, and other characteristics. When each group was asked to read each text, Anderson discovered that individuals read more skillfully, more accurately, and with better recall when they read the text that dealt specifically with their culture. Anderson's conclusion, Hirsch reported, was that reading is more than just a linguistic skill; it "involves translinguistic knowledge beyond the abstract sense of words" ("Cultural Literacy," p. 165). Hence, the assumptions of educational formalism—that skills can be taught independent of prescribed content or context—were shown to be incorrect.

This will all seem reasonably obvious to the nonacademic observer, but one must recall the fervor for skill-based education at that time. The nonacademic observer should also be aware that great steps must sometimes be taken to correct established error simply because it is established. Hirsch floated his ideas in a number of forums for some time before the actual publication of *Cultural Literacy*. The quote in the previous paragraph, for example, actually comes from Hirsch's article published in *The American Scholar* in 1983.

It is interesting to note that while Hirsch's writings on cultural literacy precipitated a debate, his earlier talks and essays did not attract the arrows, daggers, brickbats, and broken glass that his major trade book did. The attention given to that book presented Hirsch's opponents with a real-world problem to confront, not a tidy little debate that might be confined to convention rooms or the pages of small-circulation journals. It was unfortunate that Allan Bloom's *Closing of the American Mind: How Higher Education Has Failed Democracy and Impoverished the Souls of Today's Students* also appeared in 1987. Hirsch's book was unfairly and inappropriately paired with Bloom's in a nearly hysterical wave of counterattack.

Bloom, previously known and respected primarily as a translator and editor, was concerned with relativism in modern education and summoned all of his energies to smite it in a fit of Straussite pique. Hirsch's intentions were quite different. Unfortunately, he went on from *Cultural Literacy* to the publication of sequel material that, in some ways, trivialized the issue by moving it into the arena of how-to books. His basic conclusion, however, was not one that should occasion any great challenge: to the extent that we share a common cultural language and a common set of associations, we are better able to communicate with one another; to the extent that we lack a common heritage and a common storehouse of references, allusions, and metaphors, we will have greater difficulty communicating with one another. Thus, steps must be taken to ensure that students have some familiarity with what might reasonably be considered their common culture.

This seems simple enough. Johnson once said that classical quotation constituted the parole of literary men all over the world, linking them and facilitating discourse. "It is a good thing," he said; "there is a community of mind in it" (*Boswell's Life*, 4:102). No one, to my knowledge, greeted Johnson's view with the kind of response visited upon Hirsch. Johnson was also quick to realize that ignorance of that language would serve to further disenfranchise those most in need of what we would now call empowerment. Thus, ensuring the possession of some degree of cultural literacy could be seen as an egalitarian rather than as a hegemonic act.

In Hirsch's time, however, the politics of the situation were extremely important and pertinent questions surfaced immediately. If it were indeed useful to have a common culture, who would choose that culture? Who specifically would select the books to be taught in our schools? (Hirsch had fantasized about some national group comparable to the New York Regents.) What would be included? What would be excluded? Why should culture be thought of as fixed? Why should the list not be as fluid and varied as America itself? Why should we follow the list of books favored by previous centuries rather than our own? To what extent would inclusion on this list confer value upon the creators of the cultural artifacts? To what extent would knowledge of minority cultures both broaden the majority culture and lead to the liberation of minority populations? How do we construct a list that will protect those populations? How do we preserve our past and our cultural language while attempting to be inclusive? Is that past really worth preserving? What values does it embody? To what extent is culture really a product of power? Is the so-called canon worth preserving, since it is primarily the literature of dead, white, oppressive males?

The debate, which still continues, was extremely heated, in part because of the academic ethos in which much of it was conducted. There was little attention, for example, to such obvious facts as the extent to which "canonicity" and compulsory reading could serve to erode culture. I wonder, for example, how many students from my generation avoided all future contact with George Eliot after being force-fed *Silas Marner* in high school. I remember my own early exposure to the eighteenth century in a textbook with a chapter entitled "The Reign of Form." I assiduously avoided the period for years after reading that particular account of it.

Some years ago I was asked to review an article that subjected eighteenth-century children's books to an academic-Marxist analysis, demonstrating the manner in which these books cultivated future tools of the wealthy who could exploit their adult labor by exposing them to bourgeois propaganda in their youth. I immediately thought of Johnson's comments on those books. His view was that they were designed to be purchased by parents (much as modern dog food is scented for the purchasers, not their pets). The children themselves wanted none of that stuff; they wanted to read of blood and gore, of giants and dragons (as did Johnson). Our own time is similar. We agonize over the high politics of the school curriculum while students spend their time playing video games. (We know far less about such activities than we should, of course; Marsha Kinder has pointed out, for example, that some of these video games have generated more income—a quarter at a time—than *Gone with the Wind*. While academics do beat their breasts over their students' shortened attention spans and preference for electronic over print media, they do not begin, I fear, to appreciate the actual dimensions of the situation—the time spent in playing such games, the size of the market enjoyed by the manufacturers of such games, the values implicit in the unifying narratives of the games, the manner in which gender is inscribed within the games, and a host of other very real concerns.)

The political questions raised by the issue of cultural literacy are important and valid ones. From them have come other questions; old orthodoxies have been challenged and new orthodoxies have been advanced. The debate is real and the issues are important. However, the contexts in which the debates have transpired have largely been academic. This has materially affected the nature of those debates, and the result has been that the debates have lost contact with some important realities. Johnson once said that to a grammarian, all of the problems of the universe are reducible to problems of grammar. His own views, however—while informed by a knowledge of grammar—were far broader. Were he here, I believe he would look at other aspects of the canonicity issue.

I should say, parenthetically, that I realize that cultural literacy involves much more than canonical or common literary texts. It consists of a broad array of knowledge including references, expressions, allusions, titles, and much other information. The canonicity issue is an important subset of the larger question, but it is the issue that has been most important to the literary professoriate; hence my focusing upon it.

One important way to think of what we *ought* to read (or what we ought to be forced to read) is to consider how much there actually *is* to read and how much we realistically *can* read. Referring to interpretive practices, Hillis Miller is fond of wishing that a thousand flowers might be permitted to bloom (and their gardeners tenured). Practices are often based on particular texts. As Gerald Graff and others have pointed out, literary academics are especially enamored of those texts that validate their own particular practices. Hence, to talk of canons is also to talk of approaches to canons. We must, in short, consider what materials are available to academics and what they can realistically read, since they must deal with secondary as well as primary materials in advancing the cause of canonical primary texts for their students.

Because of their responsibilities (and because of their career aspirations), academics must read far more secondary material than their lay counterparts. The flowers that they permit to bloom have been planted by their colleagues as well as by poets, dramatists, essayists, and novelists. Thus, when we speak about these formulators (or erstwhile formulators) of the canon, we must keep in mind that they are dealing with both a scholarly canon of secondary materials and a cultural canon of primary materials.

In each case, the volume of potential material is utterly beyond intellectual control. In the United States alone, approximately fifty thousand books are published each year. Of these, approximately 750 (two books a day) are first novels. Assume—multiculturally—that we should be exposed to articles, stories, and books published beyond our own shores. The Library of Congress receives thirty-one thousand items per *day*, and much of the material there is not even catalogued. In fact, the second-largest library in the world is the corpus of uncatalogued material at the Library of Congress. The number of books published worldwide is approximately eight hundred thousand per year.

Perhaps a thousand flowers should be permitted to bloom, but that will mean that (if we forget entirely those books published abroad) 98 percent of the U.S. flowers will go unnoticed. No one can read fifty thousand books a year. Note that that is fifty thousand new books *each* year, not the number of books in print or on the shelves of libraries. To read a mere thousand books a year is to read 2.7 per day, with no vacations permitted and a schedule such as that would allow no time for reading the top thousand from previous years, previous decades, previous centuries, and other countries.

Consider the plight of the academic reader. Each year a number of scholars are asked by the editor of *Studies in English Literature* to write review-essays concerning the work that has appeared in those scholars' fields during the previous twelve-month period. One number of the journal is devoted to the Renaissance, one to the eighteenth century, and so on. For years it has been common to hear complaints from individual reviewers concerning the volume of material with which those individuals were forced to deal. Privately, people say such things as, "I'll never agree to do *that* again." Depending on the field, the number of books to be reviewed can run from four or five dozen to well over a hundred.

To do the *SEL* review is, in effect, to "keep up with one's field" for one year, and most who have done it resolve not to do it again. That assumes that one's field covers a century or so worth of English literature. In point of fact, "one's field" is now really one's research field or interests, which could be, depending on the area, more or less equivalent to the same volume of material, that is, one to three volumes of new books per week that one must take into consideration in order to participate effectively in a scholarly discussion.

Thus, university teachers of English do not "keep up" with their "teaching" fields in any empirical sense. Those who are active in research keep up with the material in their fields of research, but even to do that efficiently requires that they learn quickly how to discriminate between drivel and important material. And they do learn that. However, that means that they are forming scholarly and critical canons that parallel the canons of primary material, and those canons are, in relative terms, extremely small. What finally characterizes the behavior of literary people in universities is not so much the cultivation of large fields of flowers but more the development of one or two award-winning plants or hybrids, and that requires a narrowing of focus and a narrowing of activity rather than an expansion of either.

We should remember Montaigne's complaint that the secondary canons were already squeezing out the primary ones:

> It is more of a job to interpret the interpretations than to interpret the things, and there are more books about books than about any other subject.... The world is swarming with commentaries; of authors there is a great scarcity. (*The Complete Essays*, p. 818)

Another way of thinking about the increase of "knowledge" and temporal constraints is to consider the basic facts of life of the English curriculum. The academic year in America is generally thirty weeks in length. In one fifteen-week semester, one could assign a book a week per course, though such a reading load would be considered heavy today. Not counting the books one might read for term papers and dissertations, fifteen books per course, multiplied by five courses a semester for an undergraduate student and four courses a semester for a graduate student—for four years at each level—equals six hundred books for an undergraduate reader and 480 for a graduate, slightly over a thousand required books in eight years of postsecondary instruction.

That, of course, assumes that all that one studies is literature. A majors requirement of twenty-four credits, plus four introductory courses, would yield 180 books. Two full years of graduate coursework—a reasonable average—would yield 240.

The numbers are crude and a great deal is left out—grammar school and high school reading, extracurricular reading, and the like—but though the numbers are crude, the outlines of the overall situation are clear. Students read (and faculty teach) a relatively tiny number of books from the total number of books available. The economy of the trade necessitates the formation of canons of some sort, even for voracious readers.

The situation can be ameliorated but it cannot be significantly changed. Tutorial instruction on the British model, for example, can offer more time and more latitude for reading, but it cannot increase the number of hours in the day; and in the American system, as currently established, the institution of a largely tutorial system cannot—politically or logistically—even be contemplated.

I once did a very rough calculation of the size of the "canon" of English and American literature—the canon defined as the list of books one would need to read to make it through doctoral studies in English without significantly embarrassing oneself. Needless to say, one would read deeply in fields of specialization for comprehensive examinations, but the overall list—comparable, let us say, to a tough, master's-level recommended list—was about six hundred volumes. Reading a hundred pages a day (while also attending classes, doing papers, and taking examinations) would yield seven hundred pages a week, or approximately three books. That would be 3.85 years of reading, with no holidays or vacations permitted, and a good bit more than the 420 books read by my imaginary student taking a standard undergraduate English major and two full years of graduate coursework.

My list of six hundred books contained no secondary material. It referred only to primary, literary texts. Graduate students, however, and an increasing number of undergraduates often focus a significant portion of their attention on secondary materials. The farther scholars get from graduate school, the more they tend to read secondary materials (particularly new secondary materials) because they must reread certain primary materials as part of class preparation and their career demands will press them to stay abreast of the ongoing scholarly dialogue so that they can continue to participate in it.

Canon formation, of some sort, is thus a necessity, and the number of flowers permitted to bloom must be carefully managed to ensure that curricular responsibilities and career demands are met. That does not mean that there will not be new ideas, new texts, and new perspectives. What it means is that they must fit a template mandated by the economies of the profession, the requirements of educational institutions and governing bodies, and the realities of the publishing industry.

One might imagine a vast cultural war with texts, charges, and countercharges hurled back and forth like the mountains in the heavenly battle of Book 6 of *Paradise Lost*, but the reality is that canons come to us already formed. By the time a trade book comes into our hands, it has been read by one or more agents' assistants, one or more agents, one or more editors, and a number of pre- and postpublication reviewers. By the time a university press book comes into our hands, it has been read by one or more prepublication reviewers, an acquisitions editor, a member of the press board, and a number of reviewers.

All of these individuals are filters. They determine what we shall read. When we make our selections from the fifty thousand books published each year in the United States, we pay attention to such things as the previous work of the author, the reputation of the publisher, and the nature of the reviews and reviewers who have screened the material for us. Perhaps most of all we listen to the scholarly equivalent of word-of-mouth. We see which books are being read and cited most frequently, and we secure them for ourselves. If we did not, we could not participate in the scholarly discussion/debate.

My point is that that list of books is infinitesimally small—just like the list of books reviewed in major organs such as the *New York Times*, the *Washington Post Book World*, or the *Times Literary Supplement*. Many books are never advertised and many are never reviewed. They simply disappear into the abyss. In large measure, those books that we do read have been rendered canonical (or semicanonical) by a series of intellectual and economic filters that stand between us and the author.

Some will come to our attention because of the remarks of one or two important reviewers. Some will be given notoriety by what Fish calls interpretive communities. Some will be noted a year or two later as we scan citation indices. Some will actually be advertised, and some will be praised or damned by word of mouth. Some will even be the subject of extensive discussion in scholarly forums, like Hirsch's book, but no matter how these books come to our attention, the number that actually comes to our attention will be small.

Once books gain sufficient applause and notoriety, they will be read widely. Individuals will encourage colleagues and force students to read them also. They will become a part of the debate—a part of the scholarly canon. That canon may have a shorter lifespan than the canon of primary materials, but it is very important, since critical and scholarly attitudes help to shape the canon of primary materials by raising the stock of particular authors and works therein.

It must be remembered, however, that the debate that will center on key texts must be manageable, since the careers of the participants depend upon it. The debate yields the publications upon which promotions and merit increments turn, so it must be kept to human scale. Northrop Frye once compared the disputed territory of the battles within literary theory to Fortinbras's field of operations in *Hamlet*, arguing that it was barely sufficient to contain the combatants ("Literary and Linguistic Scholarship in a Postliterate World," p. 991). This is, in fact, the ideal battlefield for the literary academic—small enough to be logistically controllable, complex enough to keep laypeople beyond its boundaries.

If secondary text canons must be kept to a manageable size, so too must primary text canons. We are bound by the number of hours in the day, the number of courses required for a degree, the number of weeks in the semester or quarter, and, increasingly, by the titles that are currently in print. Canons and curricula change, of course. Titles are added and titles drop off, but the requirement that there be a manageable list continues. Thus, when we speak of "opening up the canon," we are not talking about dropping the English Renaissance and adding the work of all women writers from Argentina. We are talking about incremental changes or substitutions within a fluid list of books that is perforce extremely small. A prominent African American critic recently lamented the fact that while a significant number of English courses at a major university now included the works of African American writers, the great majority of instructors were teaching the same book: Zora Neale Hurston's *Their Eyes Were Watching God*. This might occasion concern, but given the nature of the trade it should not occasion surprise.

A number of other factors affect the canon of primary materials. There is, for example, the phenomenon of an official canon and a *de facto* canon. Many great books are not taught because they are unteachable. They are still described as canonical, but virtually no one now reads them. How would one, for example, teach Chapman's or Pope's translations of Homer to contemporary students who study in fifteen-week time bites and do not read Greek? Dickens has often been represented by the shorter *Hard Times* rather than *Our Mutual Friend*, *Little Dorrit*, or *Bleak House* because of curricular or temporal restraints. Whole periods may be "mistaught," "misrepresented," or inappropriately filtered because the period's major works are unteachable. Many undergraduate students of the Restoration and eighteenth century, for example, will not have been asked to read or use Pope's Homer, Johnson's Dictionary, Gibbon's *Decline and Fall*, Newton's *Principia*, Hume's *Treatise of Human Nature*, or—increasingly— Swift's *Tale of a Tub* because they are either too long or too recondite.

Many writers have been encountered through commentators (Kant, Hegel, Wittgenstein, Heidegger, Derrida, for example), while others lend themselves to more direct reading (Locke, Nietzsche, Barthes, Foucault, or A. J. Ayer). Much of the "canon," no matter whose canon it is, comes to us predigested and filtered. The more difficult the individual canonical text, the smaller will be the total number of canonical texts.

The bottom line is that no matter which trench you inspect during the cultural wars, you will continue to find the same texts in the combatants' rucksacks. That is because of the economy of the university, the economy of the profession, human mortality, and the human need for sleep.

There is another phenomenon here, which at first glance appears to be an exception to more common patterns. A number of individuals study materials that are largely unfamiliar to the majority of those individuals' readers. They study, in short, noncanonical texts. Such studies are often cultural rather than literary or philosophic, the scholar drawing conclusions with regard to society from a large class of materials and not focusing on one or more time-honored or heavily vetted texts. However, these studies themselves often become canonical because most readers look to the writer of the study to filter those materials for them.

For example, Leslie Fiedler's *Love and Death in the American Novel* looks at a number of noncanonical texts, but Fiedler's book itself is a text with which the great majority of literary academics are familiar. Jane Tompkins offers a serious look at Louis L'Amour in her book *West of Everything: The Inner Life of Westerns*. No matter how popular with real-world readers, none of L'Amour's many books are canonical within the academy. However, because of the academy's lack of familiarity with L'Amour (and because of the academy's familiarity with Jane Tompkins), Tompkins's book is becoming canonical for *literary* students of American popular culture. At the same time, it will probably not become canonical for film students who focus on American popular culture, because the range of films that the book considers is far too narrow and because film students have a more sophisticated knowledge of popular genres than most literary students. The same is true of a book like John G. Cawelti's *Adventure, Mystery, and Romance: Formula Stories as Art and Popular Culture*, which is very useful and even canonical for literary students, but not for film students, and far too elementary for passionate readers of genre fiction, who, each week, consume books by the armful.

Such readers are far closer to Johnson in their practices than they are to academic readers, one of the great differences between Johnson and modern literary commentators being the simple breadth of his reading. Johnson is not a fair measure or norm since, in Adam Smith's opinion, he knew more books than any man alive. Even more distinctive in Johnson's case is the fact that he read in a multiplicity of areas, including popular writing. Milton knew a great many books also, but few can match Johnson in catholicity. His taste for romances and fairy tales (the latter of which he also wrote) has already been mentioned; he also read widely in religion, theology, philosophy, history, law, language, literature, numismatics, science, medicine, geography, travel, education, economics, biography, and what we would term popular crafts. He was, in his practices, far closer to the modern popular reader than to the modern scholarly reader. His reading is more that of the intense amateur, not the narrow scholar. It is also the reading of a journalist and book reviewer, which, among many other things, he was.

One is now struck by the amount of scorn heaped upon journalists by denizens of the academy. "Journalistic" is a term of opprobrium, applied to writing that is descriptive rather than theoretical. In some ways this is understandable; academic disciplines define themselves through their theoretical underpinnings, and the presence or absence of theory results in the drawing (or blurring) of lines of demarcation. However, there is some notable inconsistency here and an absence of self-consciousness. For example, many of the writers whom academics teach and admire were themselves often journalists (for example, Defoe, Addison, Steele, Swift, Fielding, Johnson, Boswell, Smart, Mackenzie, Goldsmith, Burke), and many of their journalistic works continue to reward serious study.

Similarly, when we encounter academics or dryasdusts in literature, we academics tend not to prefer them. Give us the Byronic hero, not Eliot's Mr. Casaubon. When we see academics locked in combat with writers, we take the side of the writers. Down with Gabriel Harvey; give us Thomas Nashe, with his wonderful names for Harvey—Gerboduck Huddleduddle, Gilgilis Hobberdehoy, Braggadochio Glorioso, and Timothy Tiptoes.

There is something ungenerous in our views of the journalist. There may also be some envy and fear as well. Serious journalistic reviewers read far more books than academics and do far more writing. Academics may attack them for lacking a theoretical base or the specialized knowledge of a discrete research field, but the truth of the matter is that the best of them have a surer grasp of American culture than do most academics for the simple reason that they read constantly in a broad number of fields. In reprisal, academics attack the *quality* of their knowledge, but it is broad knowledge and experience that informs the cherished writings of such individuals as Johnson and Montaigne. While academics score journalists for trading in known facts and secondhand ideas, they are quite prepared to spare derivative thinkers whose works they cherish for other reasons, Coleridge, for example.

Some years ago I was sitting on a peer review panel, evaluating a set of faculty research proposals. An individual from another department reviewing the grant application of one of my colleagues said, "He is a *reader*." My immediate reaction was one of surprise; we were all readers. But of course we were not. We read materials for class and we read primary (but especially secondary) materials in our research fields. Few appeared to read passionately in English, American, or world literature, broadly conceived. The passions were professional and the energies were so channeled. There was passionate *curiosity*, and while that is good and necessary, it is not the same as passionate reading.

As I thought about the other members of my department, there was only one individual I could immediately identify as another passionate reader, but his scholarly work was largely editorial and his passionate reading was of genre fiction, principally mystery novels. On the other hand, there were several individuals I could name immediately who were passionately fond of chess or opera or symphonic music and an even greater number who were passionately interested in politics.

This situation has been complicated by the advent of intense, theoretical discourse, where a small number of texts and a small number of theorists are studied endlessly, where the validation of individual theories takes precedence over exposure to a broad and rich body of writing.

I am reminded of the father of one of my high school classmates, an expert in electronics who operated a then-state-of-the-art ham radio setup and was the first individual I encountered who had a full, component-part (as we then said) stereophonic-sound system. With his ham set, this individual communicated with people from all over the globe. I asked my classmate what his father and the other operators said to one another—what he had *learned*—and the answer was always the same: "They just discussed the kind of equipment they were using." The stereo system was an impressive one considering the time (Mary Tyler Moore was still a dancer, appearing in a famous photograph on the jacket of one of Audio Fidelity's then-popular records). I asked my classmate how many records his father actually owned. His son told me that he only had one—the old demonstration disk released by Audio Fidelity to help popularize stereophonic sound. The man was not interested in music. He was interested in the purest, most faithful reproduction of such things as railroad sounds illustrating Doppler effect. Both with his radio and his phonograph, the filtering or mediating device was far more interesting to him than the human or aesthetic realities on the other side.

Several lessons might be drawn from these anecdotes. The first is Jaroslav Pelikan's acute argument that real advances in research tend to come from general, rather than specialized, knowledge, since the specialized researcher's vision is tunneled by the canonical texts that guide his or her field. The person who brings something to bear that is not commonly possessed—knowledge from another discipline or from the outside world—is uniquely positioned to redirect the debate or dialogue, while the specialist who lacks the perspective that comes from broader knowledge continues to do Kuhnian normal science, something valued in large part because of the economy of the profession. In this mode, the activity that is considered worthwhile is that which yields more work for more workers, even if the product remains largely the same or its improvement advances slowly.

These charges should not be leveled at the theorists alone, for old-guard readers clutching their Matthew Arnold are as susceptible to the virus as new-guard (or recent new-guard) readers carrying their *Of Grammatology*. Prewar readers filter culture through Carl Becker or A. O. Lovejoy; contemporaries filter it through Clifford Geertz. The observation has been made by Denis Donoghue that contemporary critical theory consists largely of the popularization and appropriation of the thought of a small handful of individuals. Take away those few individuals and what would be left for their interpreters/followers? However, if one took away Aristotle, Plato, Horace, Longinus, Dryden, and Johnson, what shape would earlier literary study have taken and where would the old guard now turn?

The corollary to the fact that literary study has been driven by relatively small canons of primary and secondary material is Donald Davie's observation that the literary trade is one of the most difficult to practice; that is why the number of major practitioners is so small—the field has been tailored to meet the abilities of the everyday participants (p. 172). His practical point—that we turn out far too many English Ph.D.'s unequal to what should be their real task—is one of the reasons why so much literary writing is derivative and imitative. I noted above Yvor Winters's comment on the difficulty of the task of criticism and his suggestion that the only writer capable of meeting it was Samuel Johnson. Harold Bloom has said much the same thing. In Colin Campbell's famous "Tyranny of the Yale Critics" piece, Bloom is quoted as saying, "No critic is greater than Johnson," adding, "I shall never write anything like that, alas. Alas, alas, alas" (pp. 26, 28).

Hence we study Johnson. Hence we include his texts among the canonical few. It should, moreover, be stressed that the fact that an identifiable number of individuals loom large for critics, scholars, and theorists with very different orientations suggests both the necessity of canons for academics and their students and the absurdity of holding a position that is ultimately relativist. One might argue for such a position and one's arguments might be logically unassailable, but in the world of the practicing academic, the position is indefensible.

Some critics are simply better than others. And some writers are better than others. We can wrangle endlessly over the meanings of the word *better*, but we cannot argue with the obvious. The reason that Derrida returns to Heidegger and Heidegger to Nietzsche, the reason that A. J. Ayer returns to Hume and Hume to Berkeley, the old guard to Arnold and the new guard to Bakhtin or Catherine Belsey, is very simple: these are bright people from whom they have learned, and they have learned more from them than from others. The old guard returns to Milton and Wordsworth, the new to Mallarmé and Garcia Marquez. Why? Because these are interesting writers whom they consider more interesting—better, by some measure or other—than others.

This commonsensical point crashes into the relativist's wall, one that is high and thick, with bricks contributed by varied and even diametrically opposed masons. At certain philosophic levels, relativism is extremely difficult to counter, but at the level of practice, no one can reasonably take it seriously.

Stone-kicking refutations of relativism would not be difficult. University librarians, for example, could announce severe budgetary constraints on the monograph and serials budget and invite faculty to choose between the acquisition of polarized pairs (*Being and Time*, let us say, or Rush Limbaugh's *The Way Things Ought to Be*; *New Literary History* or *Guns and Ammo*; *Signs* or *Tiger Beat*). From time to time, one might find a diehard relativist who, on principle, would refuse to choose, but that would not be a frequent occurrence.

One should also recall Fish's argument that when we doubt, we do so within a set of assumptions that cannot themselves be objects of doubt. In short, since we have to be situated somewhere, we simply cannot be complete relativists or thoroughgoing skeptics (*Is There a Text in This Class? The Authority of Interpretive Communities*, p. 360).

Ultimately, some writers speak to us more effectively than others. They may do so for a multiplicity of reasons and those reasons may change; they may even change frequently, but there *are* reasons. Regardless of our announced philosophic posture, we read selectively and, perhaps more telling, we buy selectively. Some books matter more than others. They may not matter at all to some people and they may matter more or less at different times, but some books matter more than others. That is another reason why we read and teach canonically. As Johnson might say, whatever arguments are adduced to the contrary, all practice is for it.

To "open up" the canon, to argue, for example, for a multicultural curriculum, is not to forego the need for defining traditions in which one might read new or hitherto overlooked texts. An interesting recent novel illustrates this point nicely.

Charles Johnson's novel *Middle Passage* won the National Book Award in 1990, this in the wake of the fact that three years earlier Toni Morrison's novel *Beloved*, the book of another African American writer, had been passed over both by the fiction jury for the National Book Award and the National Book Critics Circle. The fact that the Pulitzer jury honored *Beloved* with their fiction prize did not put the ethnic issues involved to rest. Immediately prior to the announcement of Johnson's receipt of the award, one of the jurors, Paul West, commented in the *New York Times* that "there is acute dividedness over nearly everything," that "ethnic concerns, ideology and moral self-righteousness" compromised what the *Washington Post* termed "considerations of merit" (Streitfeld, p. B2).

Strong words. Terry McMillan, another of the judges, accused West of making a racist and offensive statement. Two of the other fiction judges, Phillip Lopate and William Gass, the *Post* reported, "either could not be found or did not wish to comment on the record." Oh brave we. The chair of the panel, Catharine Stimpson (a former administrator as well as an English professor), said, "We had a delightful lunch. No Rolaids were served." Johnson, acquitting himself well, commented, "I don't know what to say except a little controversy is good for the soul."

We have come to expect this kind of interchange on the battlefields of the culture wars. Charges of discrimination and reverse discrimination hurtle across no-person's-land like mortar rounds, some inert, some highly explosive. And what is at stake? A great many things: recognition, *thymos*, cultural emergence, cultural dominance, cultural control, the West, the Third World, liberty, royalties, tenure. What will the canon be? What will be included? Who will be taught and who will be read?

But what of the *book* and what of its *author*? This is one of the contested areas within the culture wars, one that I will address elsewhere—the death and burial of the author and the dance of the critic-theorists upon his or her grave. It may come as no surprise that after dishing all of the academic gossip and running up the racial flag into the windy environs above the battlefield, the *Post* staff writer covering the story bollixed the novel's plot. In fact, he bollixed it on its central issue and event. Hence, one assumes that he did not read the book itself, which, some might still claim, should play at least some part in the preparations that precede the writing of a story concerning the National Book Award.

The book itself is a fascinating one and includes a number of courageous observations and interesting set pieces. Set in the nineteenth century, it concerns a recently freed slave by the name of Rutherford Calhoun. Rutherford has come from Illinois to New Orleans and has found himself in a series of difficulties that have resulted in the prospect of a forced marriage. In order to escape, Rutherford climbs aboard the slaver *Republic*, travels to Africa and back, is changed by his experiences with the white crew and the cargo of enslaved Allmuseri, is shipwrecked, saved by another ship—the *Juno*—on which is sailing his former lady friend, Isadora, and the New Orleans thug, Philippe "Papa" Zeringue, who had been holding Rutherford's markers and attempting to force him into marriage.

The book confronts a series of racial issues head-on; Rutherford, like his father, Riley Calhoun, is portrayed as a rambling good-timer, escaping responsibility for hearth and home and searching for action in various forms. His brother Jackson, on the other hand, is sweet and pious, devoted to his white master, and ready to sacrifice his legacy in the interest of higher principle. In effect, the behaviors of the brothers are consciously sketched to play to particular stereotypes.

The New Orleans thug, who is black, is later discovered to be one of the financiers of the *Republic*, his complicity in the slave ship's purposes pointing to the fact that the activity of slaving was advanced by some blacks as well as by whites. Papa Zeringue's black enforcer, Santos, has a head upon which nightsticks break—a stereotypical detail that few white novelists would dare include. Rutherford's father, Riley, is a professional victim, blaming his personal shortcomings on his "oppression." The captain of the *Republic* meets with Rutherford and quickly makes him aware of his feelings with regard to nineteenth-century anticipations of affirmative action; they are not positive.

There is, I think, a strong personal dimension to the book. As a writer and professor in what largely remains a white ethos, Johnson is able to understand many elements of the experience of his character on a deep, personal level. They are both somewhere in between. In the novel, Rutherford's white shipmates do not principally see him as black; they see him as being from Illinois, and they call him "Illinois." He is first and foremost a seaman, just as Johnson has said that he is first and foremost a writer—a black writer, indeed, but first a writer.

Similarly, the title of the novel suggests a stage in the black experience. As Rutherford functions as a cultural translator between the white seamen and the Allmuseri, Johnson—as a writer—does something of the same for his society, examining the perspectives on either side of the racial divide and, in several senses of the term, mediating. He is reminiscent of several of the major eighteenth-century writers, Samuel Johnson in particular, who moved among the rich and who also moved among the poor, among the masters and among the servants, among the members of the peerage, the merchant class, and professions, among the industrious poor (as they were sometimes termed) and the lost underclass, interpreting culture and society from a unique vantage point.

Middle Passage is a deeply American book, confronting a defining experience for African Americans, but it confronts that experience from a multiplicity of perspectives, some of them quite conservative. At the same time, it is an adventure novel, and while one might get through it with little so-called cultural literacy, the book is written within a set of contexts that are clearly purposeful. One could hardly imagine a novel that makes greater use of the established literary canon as a frame of reference.

Originally titled *Rutherford's Travels*, the Swiftian echo parallels the Defoan: Rutherford Calhoun/Robinson Crusoe, though in his abilities as a successful survivor Rutherford suggests Moll Flanders as well as Robinson (or, later, Ishmael). The ship's first mate takes his

Canons and Culture Wars

quips from Samuel Johnson, saying that, "Being on a ship *is* being in jail with the chance of being drowned to boot" (p. 25).

The African American novelist David Bradley commented in his jacket blurb that "*Middle Passage* is as fatalistic as *The Rime of the Ancient Mariner*, funny as *Gulliver's Travels*, exciting as *Treasure Island*, metaphorical as *Robinson Crusoe*, and memorable as them all." There are obvious echoes of *Moby Dick*, of the *Odyssey*, of Tennyson's "Ulysses," and of the *Ship of Fools* (both Brandt's and Katherine Anne Porter's). The book is built upon both the picaresque and bildungsroman traditions. The orlop deck in the bowels of the *Republic* is half-Chaucer, half-Dante; at one point Rutherford (educated by his white master, the Reverend Chandler) refers to the Wife of Bath's tale. He also remarks that his lady, Isadora Bailey, speaks in choriams and iambs and he notes the fact that in their drama, the Greeks preferred to keep their violence offstage. Rutherford speaks of the "Byronic sigh," and Johnson has one of his shipmates discuss El Greco and Rubens. That particular character is later eaten, sacramentally, as in the Piers Paul Read account of the Andes crash, *Alive*, and the depiction of the colossus below decks is pure, contemporary magic realism.

The paranoid captain, Ebenezer Falcon, with his explosive devices, room traps, and magnetized gun, is part Captain Queeg, part Commander Bond, and the kicker ending—in which the enforcer Santos turns on the New Orleans thug rather than on Rutherford (because Santos learns of Papa's complicity in the slaving operation and Santos himself is an Allmuseri)—is pure Elmore Leonard. The timing, the surprise resolution that remains plausible, recalls in particular Leonard's *Killshot*.

In short, Charles Johnson is, in *Middle Passage*, a black writer writing a very white book on a subject of compelling importance to both black and white Americans. This is not an academic book in the sense that the art novel is, but it is an English teacher's book with complicating symbols and allusions as far as the academic eye can see. Rutherford's *cri de coeur* in the midst of tumult ("I'm not on *anybody's* side! I'm just trying to keep us *alive!*" [p. 137]) may be Johnson's as well.

The book exhibits the kind of cultural and intellectual ambidexterity that Keats prized and illustrates the fact that a book by an African American writer dealing with slavery can also be written deeply within (and take significant leverage from) a predominantly white literary tradition. Indeed, African American writers have traditionally worked within a multiplicity of traditions. The book also stands in interesting contrast to the wrangling of the ideologues, not just concerning its receipt of the National Book Award, but within the culture wars generally. It confronts racial issues without trepidation; it relies on deep literary and popular traditions, and it is written for both a literary and a popular audience. While the culture wars were raging around him, a skilled writer was writing a very good book, diverting our attention from the academic conflicts—thankfully—and helping us, in the process, to put the debates concerning tradition and innovation into a more sophisticated and nuanced perspective.

We cannot understand ourselves without understanding the traditions of which we are a part, and in many cases—certainly in the case of a book like *Middle Passage*—we cannot understand other traditions or views without understanding the tradition with which virtually all living writers have some serious contact. It is difficult to select an adjective to describe that tradition. "Standard" suggests a norm against which other traditions have to be measured, and that is imprecise. "Dominant" suggests a hegemonic status that is equally imprecise.

Dominance also suggests a degree of coherence and commonality that cannot really be demonstrated. If the standard (or dominant, or "western") tradition *controls*, who or what is doing the controlling? Consider, for example, the most influential poem in English: *Paradise Lost*. Whom or what does Milton speak for? Johnson confronts this question at length in his *Life of Milton*. He admires Milton's great poem, but he loathes Milton's politics. Similarly, he scores Milton for his "Turkish contempt of females, as subordinate and inferior beings" (*Life of Milton, Lives*, 1:157). He says of Milton's religion that "we know rather what he was not, than what he was" (1:155), though Johnson is well aware of Milton's strong anti-Catholicism.

Was Milton a defender of the status quo, of the "dominant culture"? Hardly. As Latin secretary to Cromwell, part of his job was to justify the execution of Charles I to continental Europe. Executing a king may be many things; one thing it is not is a defense of the status quo. Milton does not speak for Anglicans. He does not speak for Tories. He does not speak for men in his views of women. He most certainly does not speak for Catholics. He does not speak for England in any decisive political or religious way.

But who does stand for the status quo, who does protect cultural hegemony against the incursions of the outsider? Chaucer criticizes his culture, including his church. Shakespeare is often quite elusive in his personal attitudes and values, but many of his views are forward-looking, for example his strong criticism of the manner in which women are objectified and "valued" by men in *Troilus and Cressida* (the principal point of the play, Bob Ornstein stressed to us in the pre-revolutionary days of 1963–64). Spenser is a defender of his church and country, sometimes a rigidly anti-Catholic one, but he has women heroines and he includes them as more than simply sops to Elizabeth. Moreover, in Andrew Weiner's reading, there is a heavily Christian, antimartial thrust to the *Faerie Queene* that serves to elevate sacrifice over war, and while it would not please Nietzsche, it would certainly please many of the children of the 1960s.

Donne? Which one, mad Jack or the Dean of St. Paul's? Dryden? Which one, the supporter of Cromwell or the supporter of the restored Stuart king? Pope and (the later) Swift, the Tory satirists? If the Tories are hegemonic, then what must we do about Defoe, Addison, Steele, Burke, and the other Whigs? Richardson is hardly a defender of the status quo; he is one of the chief initiators of a revolutionary change in the perception of the relations between men and women. Fielding the novelist had much more tolerance than Fielding the judge. Was Hume a conservative? Perhaps in his views of English history, but not in his philosophy and not in his willingness to sacrifice personal advantage and academic sinecures in the interest of saying what he believed.

Was Gibbon a traditionalist? Certainly not in his views of Christianity, the chapters on which were sometimes excised by binders of his *Decline and Fall* to save the sensibilities of the pious. Was Blake (in Erdman's phrase a "prophet against empire") a supporter of British adventuring? Johnson (like Richard Savage and Oliver Goldsmith) also had a good bit to say about empire building and colonialism, and it is consistently and notoriously harsh.

The young Wordsworth? Byron? Shelley? DeQuincey the opium eater? Mary Wollstonecraft? Mill and Bentham? Dickens ("damned radical," in Soames Forsyte's phrase)? Jane Austen, with her "regulated hatred"? George Eliot? The Brontës, with Charlotte the creator of the madwoman in the attic who haunts Jean Rhys's and every contemporary feminist's imagination? Oscar Wilde? Strachey? Hardy? Conrad? Forster, Keynes, Virginia Woolf, and the rest of the Bloomsbury group? Lawrence (D. H. *or* T. E.)? Shaw? Joyce? Orwell? Auden? Larkin?

Where are the defenders of the status quo? Where are the traditionalists? Where are the preservers of cultural hegemony? There are individuals with traditionalist sides (Yeats, for example), even fascist sympathizers (Pound) and individuals with distasteful or even disgusting associations who yet win the defense of the countercultural (Heidegger, Paul de Man), but where are the reasonably consistent defenders of the status quo? Locke? Certainly Voltaire did not see him in that light. James Boswell? Even Boswell cavorted with ne'er-do-wells like Wilkes and broke windows in the streets of Edinburgh to protest court decisions. Perhaps Arnold, but not consistently so.

And the great writers of America? Thoreau? Melville? Hawthorne? Emily Dickinson? (Worse yet, Camille Paglia's Emily Dickinson?) Whitman? Willa Cather? Fitzgerald? Stevens? Cummings? Crane? Faulkner? Steinbeck? Kerouac? Ginsberg? O'Hara? Baldwin? Plath? Baraka? Eliot, possibly, but far from consistently. James, possibly, but in very special ways.

The writers who have mattered most to us tend to share one thing in common: opposition to the status quo and the frequent desire to challenge cultural, political, religious, and, yes, in many cases, heterosexual hegemony. There is also a good deal of generational competition among the writers themselves, but again, that does not constitute coherence, commonality, and a united front in defense of the established; quite the opposite.

But is this quite heterogeneous canon not possessed by individuals in such a way as to result in actions that constitute a form of hegemony? Are not certain texts taught time and again and are not certain attitudes inculcated time and again? Are we not force-feeding and indoctrinating, crowding multicultural possibilities from the minds of our students in the interest of maintaining some increasingly distant tradition?

Somewhere someone is probably attempting to do that. There are people who fail to see the countercultural dimensions of virtually all great writing, who tame the texts and the texts' authors, making them manageable and compliant. Who are these demons?

> There is a tendency in the scholarly writing done by professors and composers of theses that sometimes becomes rather exasperating to the reader outside the college world. This tendency may be briefly described as an impulse on the part of the professors to undermine their subjects or explain them away....
>
> In order to understand this peculiar phenomenon which it seems to me has been growing more formidable, one must understand, first of all, the relation of the professor to his subjects. This relation is, nine times out of ten, a strained and embarrassing one. The professor would be made most uncomfortable if he had to meet Whitman or Byron; he would not like him—he does not, in fact, like him. But he has gone in for studying literature and he must try to do something to advance himself in that field. (Edmund Wilson, "Reëxamining Dr. Johnson," p. 13)

The culture wars are, in large measure, an academic phenomenon. The stakes are determined by the combatants, and they are socially, culturally, and professionally constructed far more than they are real. There are surely many possessors of my six-hundred-book canon, the vast majority among the professoriate, but how great are their numbers, particularly in terms of larger demographics?

In 1990–91 1,416 doctoral degrees were awarded in the broad area of letters, a mere 3.6 percent of the 39,294 doctorates. Nearly twice as many professional degrees were earned (71,948) as all of the Ph.D.'s combined. Possessors of postbaccalaureate degrees (of all stripes) represent only 7.2 percent of the U.S. population. Assuming, fairly, I believe, that undergraduate majors do not "possess" the canon after the handful of courses they have taken, the possessors would be limited to a few brave autodidacts and some possessors of doctoral degrees in letters. Taking two thousand such individuals per year (a generous estimate) and multiplying by fifty (again, being generous: using a figure of eight to ten years to complete a Ph.D., fifty years would take the possessors past life expectancy averages), we have approximately one hundred thousand people from whose ranks we could recruit the protectors of the white phallologocentric tradition, dedicated to the task of protecting their supposed hegemony. Current estimates place the number of U.S. citizens who speak a language other than English at home at 13.8 percent of the population. In other words, against this (very generously estimated) hundred-thousand-strong, fusty army of potential phallologocentrists, we have a population of approximately thirty-five million who, at home at least, are not speaking that army's language. My point is that beyond the cultural wars lie other things of an educational and cultural nature that are deserving of attention on the part of the nation's teachers of literature. The educated general public *does* care about canons and canonicity, but they care about many other things as well, as indeed they (and we) should.

The *Washington Post* reported on September 9, 1993, that approximately ninety million adults in our society are incapable of performing elementary tasks in reading, writing, and computation. The next morning the *Post* reported a lack of correlation between educational results (measured by SAT scores) and per-pupil dollar expenditures. The very real political, economic, and educational problems facing our society so diminish the problems that so often occupy the academy that we should not be surprised that the larger society is often tempted to lose heart.

Over a decade ago during an English department meeting at a distinguished private university, one of that department's leading scholars told his colleagues that they must come to realize one simple fact: that the vast number of their students' parents have sacrificed in order to pay that school's high tuition for one important reason—to ensure that their children would never have to work with their hands. He then went on to say that those parents respected research and would encourage research, but that the *quid pro quo* was the education of their children. His colleagues were chagrined by that statement. Now, years later, there might be more sympathy (perhaps even respect) expressed for the individuals who work with their hands, but the warning stands. In *The Death of Literature* (p. 201), Alvin Kernan notes that there are now departments of communications that might take on the task of education in language and composition and utterly marginalize departments of English by taking away one of their principal reasons for being.

I do not bring this up here to reopen the false dichotomy of teaching versus research; my point concerns political realities and the extent to which they are perceived by the academy. The cultural wars were important in several exemplary ways, but their overall importance is utterly dwarfed by the political realities around them. Moreover, the relative inattention that those political realities received from the literary combatants is a matter of some moment.

Assuming, of course that the wars over the canon actually *did* occur. (What?) Nearly every year the national press is unable to resist the temptation to report on the sessions held at the annual meeting of the Modern Language Association, holding the more extreme examples up to public ridicule, often by simply listing the sessions' published titles. MLA officials in turn respond by saying that these annual stories are the result of exaggeration and the failure of the laity to appreciate the nature of serious scholarship. In short, they attempt to blow off the charges. They do not confront the issue head-on. The real point (which they would never confront) is that the more flammable matters discussed (race, class, sexual orientation, and so on) are of great importance. Our society *recognizes* that they are of great importance. The problem is the dull, imitative, careerist, and politically predictable ways in which they are addressed by a significant number of the speakers. The problem is not in the issues; the problem is in what is done with these issues within the context of the economy of the profession. And *that* the MLA is not anxious to address because the association itself is a part of that economy, making money on a large convention that people will attend because they can read papers there and earn credits toward promotion and merit increments. In this regard, as in most others, the organization is less an agent for change than it is a direct reflection of the lowest common denominator of the membership.

Similarly, when conservative National Endowment for the Humanities or Office of Education officials fire off reports on the canon or the general curriculum, the MLA characteristically responds that these commentaries are also much exaggerated, that, in fact, surveys show that the traditional canon is largely intact, that it has simply been enriched (see, for example, Applebome).

I believe that that is largely true, though my own evidence is the surveying of required textbooks in the college and university bookstores I visit. The world has not fallen apart. The canon—defined as those books that we read and regularly teach—has been expanded and it has been enriched. It is a pity it did not happen sooner.

I will return to some of these issues later. My point here is that the

MLA places itself in the odd position of structuring annual conventions with an array of sessions that send one set of messages. Then, when they are under attack, they say, "Not to worry. Things have really not changed that much." In other words, those new thrusts in scholarship to which we seem to be committed blood, bone, and marrow are not having any impact that should occasion concern. The culture wars, the canon debates, the push for a new curriculum have been hideously exaggerated; the parents, taxpayers, foundations, and governmental agencies should kick back, take comfort, and continue to write checks.

And perhaps they are right. The only clear manner in which the curricula have changed is in their offering of new and/or relatively unconstrained choices (or increased incoherence, depending on your point of view). Many talks have been given in many convention rooms and many papers have been published, but most are so formulaic, imitative, and predictable that their overall results have been minimal in relation to their numbers. What has been said is relatively unthreatening because basically the same things are said over and over. A second point that should be noted is that the potential political impact of the individuals involved is radically reduced because of those individuals' notions of politics and political action.

The case of the nomination of Carol Iannone to the Humanities Council has been discussed endlessly, and I will not belabor it. I will only make the point that the marshalling of opposition to that appointment indicates the kind of "political" issue that is capable of energizing the academic literary establishment. Forget the ninety million adults who have difficulty reading, writing, and counting; here is something important—a possible effect on grant proposal decisions at the federal agency whose resources most directly affect scholarship in the humanities.

While it is both human and prudent to be concerned about such matters, the absence of MLA and other group responses *commensurate with* the enormity of other educational and cultural issues speaks volumes. In other places and in other times, literary writers and intellectuals have played a quite different role within their societies. The MLA itself is a subject beyond my concerns here, though one might reasonably ask why such a large professional organization studiously avoids such basic political activities as lobbying. I once asked an individual sympathetic to that organization why the MLA does not either locate in Washington and get down to real political business or locate in the Midwest or South where costs are far lower than in Manhattan and either lower dues (thus enlarging membership and welcoming those most in need who cannot currently afford to join) or increase services to the current membership. The individual to whom I directed the question answered, "Well, Dick, wouldn't *you* rather live in New York?" The answer said it all. Before a society worries about making a decent provision for its poor, it must worry about the accommodations of its guardians.

3

ARE ADDISON AND STEELE DEAD?

In 1990 Brian McCrea published a book entitled *Addison and Steele Are Dead: The English Department, Its Canon, and the Professionalization of Literary Criticism*. It is a courageous book, for McCrea argues a number of points that, because of their truth, are unlikely to win many academic friends. Some samples:

> The English department succeeded insofar as it established its worth without any appeal to social relevance. (p. 16)

> The ultimate step in the aggrandizement of any professional group is for its members to get paid to talk about how they do what they do rather than doing it. (p. 17)

> Recent criticism will entertain almost any question of meaning but will not entertain any question of value. (p. 140)

I hesitate to summarize briefly a book as rich as this, but McCrea's basic thesis is as follows: Addison and Steele are too clear and plainspoken to meet the needs of the English profession, which requires crabbed, complex texts to interpret in order to justify its continued existence. To the extent that texts do not require the mediation of the professor, they fall out of the canon into a textual limbo, regardless of their inherent strengths and regardless of their relevance to other human concerns.

There are many corollaries to this point, some of which McCrea traces in detail. The book is, for example, a general reflection on Graff's (and others') point that members of the English trade seek out texts that validate their personal theoretical postures. The alternative, one noted by Graff and increasingly by many others, would be to allow the text to call forth the theory (or approach) most suitable to *it*, rather than that which is most suitable to the needs and interests of the mediating English professor, a critical posture most often associated with the work of R. S. Crane. I will return to this issue later.

For McCrea, the problem is more general. Contemporary theories of all stripes are affected by professional concerns. The principal professional concern is self-justification and survival. Hence—regardless of the particular theoretical approaches of the moment—the profession's principal requirement for any text is ambiguity. That ambiguity sets what McCrea calls "interpretive challenges," which then call forth the special expertise of the professional. "Subtlety" and "complexity" will do as well, because the English profession—like other professions—seeks to control access to its ranks by excluding the nonprofessional (translation: journalists). Contemporary theory does very nicely in this regard since it also calls for a specialized language and a particular set of specialized skills. Fortunately, these can be learned rather easily and the professional can then employ them to advance his or her career.

From this, one might assume that the English profession is engaged in an economic exercise, restricting access in order to control its numbers and thus keep its market value high. That, however, is not the case. Admission requirements for graduate study in English are not restrictive in the manner, for example, of veterinary science, which—because of the limited number of places—is perhaps the most difficult to enter of currently existing professions. Rather, as with law schools, there is a sliding scale of institutions that offer doctoral work in English, and nearly anyone with the grit to stay the course of a program can find a program to which he or she can be admitted.

Nor does the profession restrict access by requiring particularly extensive knowledge from its students. It requires a good bit of knowledge, but the sheer quantity is not nearly as daunting as the required material of other programs. For example, graduate programs such as those in musicology make far greater demands: knowledge of musical notation, knowledge of medieval Latin, knowledge of French, German, and Italian (minimally), and knowledge of world music from Adam to the present.

Without arguing for a return to a purely historical approach to literary study, it must be realized that such an approach potentially makes far greater demands on students than a theory-based approach, which enjoys the capability of narrowing the canon to those texts that serve to validate the local professoriate's favored theories. One of the attractive features of New Historicist and "cultural studies" approaches to literature is that such approaches should widen the canon or the material for study rather than narrow it. Students who undertake such an approach will, simply, have to know more.

With regard to the long-term needs of the profession *qua* profession, elevated requirements would be of benefit. If English professors always *did* know more than others (journalists, for example) they would be more useful to society; if the requirements for access to their profession involved the acquisition of a sufficient degree of knowledge to narrow the profession's ranks, then the salaries and status of the members of the profession should—assuming normal circumstances—rise. Given the fact that people in the humanities often suffer from a largely self-inflicted inferiority complex (the general public *does* care about and value what they do), a heightened set of expectations might lead to increased self-esteem, greater personal happiness, and more effective professional performance.

This has not, however, generally been the approach that has been taken, since smaller ranks would bring side effects that some consider negative. For example, a smaller number of graduate students would mean a smaller number of graduate seminars for the professoriate to offer. A smaller number of graduate students would mean a smaller number of teaching assistants. A smaller number of professors would mean a smaller Modern Language Association and a smaller number of registrations at their annual convention.

Instead, we have opted for the large program/sliding scale approach. The 1982 Associated Research Councils' survey of doctoral programs evaluated 106 such programs in English language and literature. By the 1993 survey there were 127 programs evaluated. The difference in admission standards and, perforce, the requirements that can realistically be enforced vary markedly across a wide spectrum of departments. Hence, the outcomes distribute across a wide spectrum. Because the graduates of those programs will compete for positions in over thirty-six hundred institutions, it is clear that they will find themselves in career paths so different in nature as to be incomparable.

Teachers in most of those thirty-six hundred institutions will, essentially, be high school teachers, teaching multiple sections of composition and introductory literature courses to students in need of remedial work. Others (far fewer in number) will teach specialized courses in their field and research area to a small number of students, many at the graduate level. Most will fall somewhere in between, and there may be no correlation between the quality of a student's preparation and the nature of the job that that student actually secures. In seller's market times (for example, between Sputnik and the mid-1960s), young Ph.D.'s with little taste or aptitude for research found themselves in major research institutions; in buyer's market times (1969 forward, with a recent, exceptional blip), a large number of able individuals have found themselves in institutions whose needs and expectations were at variance with their personal professional ambitions.

I do not wish to return here to the problems generated by a profession that trains (or attempts to train) individuals to do narrow research but whose members largely spend their professional lives doing something else. The numerous dislocations resulting from the present realities are well known. The point that I would make is that things could be very different than they are and that the profession has done comparatively little to effect those changes that it is actually capable of effecting. It has not, for example, set and enforced standards (for itself, for its students) of the sort that it should be uniquely positioned to establish. (The MLA is shamed, for example, by the practices in this regard of the American Chemical Society.) Rather, it has tended to opt for proliferation and spread (in programs, in subject matter, in scholarly journals) rather than confronting and making difficult decisions, and it has tended to follow the practices of a few leaders (wherever those leaders might take them) rather than decide upon profession-wide norms and standards as a large, professional body. In effect, the MLA has far less impact on the profession than does the work of a tiny handful of individuals. Nietzsche would be proud.

Essentially, the English profession has attempted to practice an elitist activity in an egalitarian fashion. We continue to aspire to high standards (taking as our models a few major thinkers), but we have no qualms about increasing the number of aspirants. This results, all too often, in a profession of imitators rather than a society of *"profess*ors," each known for his or her special approach to the field. As McCrea documents, we have moved away from the preprofessional "celebrity" period of the trade to a phase in which a strategy of leveling has displaced a strategy that prizes individuality and personality. McCrea mentions, for example, that scion of an earlier age, William Lyon Phelps, priding himself on teaching four hundred students a year, in contrast to his modern counterparts who pride themselves on their ability to teach few or no students (*Addison and Steele*, p. 151). He mentions Wilbur Cross who retired from Yale, was elected to four terms as governor of Connecticut, and edited the *Yale Review* while he was in office (p. 152). He gives the instructive example of Leslie Fiedler:

> He remains, for me, probably the most interesting academic critic writing today because his acculturation, while powerful, has been incomplete. He walks among us like an intellectual dinosaur—a William Lyon Phelps stranded in the professional era. (p. 169)

I will return to Fiedler later. His experience is interesting from a number of points of view, and I believe that his practices are instructive as we attempt to chart future tendencies. Here, however, I would like to take McCrea's argument a step further and ask whether or not Addison and Steele are truly dead. To the extent that they are, we can see the price that the profession has been willing to pay in return for their demise.

The eighteenth century contributed two major forms to English literature: the novel and the periodical essay. The success of the first is ongoing; the second—in its original form—has largely disappeared. The two forms evolved together and were directed at a common audience. Recently, Paul Hunter has shown how the early novel developed, in part, from a number of pre-novelistic forms and activities, the novel meeting many of the needs that were addressed by late Renaissance how-to books, often published in periodical form.

Hunter's work recalls Louis B. Wright's famous book on middle-class culture in Elizabethan England, a discussion of the bourgeois counterparts to Castiglione's famous *Il Cortegiano*. These materials helped prepare an emerging group, a group in possession of sterling but lacking knowledge and confidence, to take their place within English society. The novel, in good measure, according to Hunter, speaks to the same need as the how-to book, offering social capital to its readers. It portrays people and describes circumstances of direct and real concern to those readers. What, for example, should a poor but able woman in service do if her master makes sexual overtures? How can she protect her virtue as well as her position? What did Richardson's Pamela do?

One of the principal pre-novelistic works cited by Hunter is a work that also dramatically affected the periodical essay tradition: John Dunton's *Athenian Gazette or Casuistical Mercury*, the title later shortened to the *Athenian Mercury*. This was one of many projects initiated by Dunton, a fascinating, eccentric late-seventeenth-century bookseller. Beginning publication on March 17, 1691, and running for more than half a decade, the *Athenian Mercury* began as a weekly but was quickly published twice weekly. Purporting to offer the services of the august membership of the Athenian Society—which would answer the weightiest of questions posed by Dunton's readership—the society actually consisted of Dunton himself and two brothers-in-law with additional help from Dr. John Norris, rector of Bemerton. One of those brothers-in-law was Samuel Wesley, father of Charles and John Wesley.

While the society entertained questions on various topics, it issued individual numbers devoted to specific topics. Its success was enormous, Dunton effectively duping some of the powerful and famous at the same time that he offered useful advice and information to members of the middle class. In Dunton—and in the immensely influential Addison and Steele, who learned the lesson of Dunton's success well—we have the first extended appeal to and involvement of the audience in an undertaking that aspired to offer instruction but could also be (or also degenerate into) entertainment.

In short, this is the origin of interactive entertainment in its recognizably modern form. Phil Donahue once said that the strength of his talk show lay in the fact that he went beyond the activities on stage and capitalized on the wisdom and energy of his audience. Dunton, however, was there first, and while his invention was designed to respond to the most serious of questions, that same design opened the door to the possibility of the periodical's sudden degeneration into a domestic advisor or worse. We are, at the outset, only a step away from the Royal Society's *Philosophical Transactions* on the one hand and a step away from Ann Landers and Geraldo Rivera on the other.

We are also but a step away from talk radio and Rush Limbaugh. Given the importance of electronic interactions for contemporary politics (and the desire of both Ross Perot and the Clinton administration to increase those possibilities), it is clear that the origins of this activity should be of more than passing interest, particularly if one asks such questions as, how difficult is it to sustain a serious level of discourse in such a setting? Or, is it inevitable—as in Dunton, Defoe, Addison, Steele, and their endless line of successors—that the risk be ever present, indeed often irresistible, that the interactions themselves become the subject, rather than the questions asked, and the activity quickly become a source of entertainment alone rather than, primarily, a source of instruction?

Needless to say, politics has long been more a source of entertainment than a source of instruction, but as we move into more complex forms of interaction—negotiating the passing lanes on the data superhighways and bouncing about in cyberspace—it becomes far more interesting and potentially far more important to study the origins of such activities, the needs they were designed to serve, the methods they used, and the results they actually achieved. To the extent that our professional posture marginalizes such figures as Addison and Steele, we are less able to understand crucial aspects of our own experience, both cultural and political.

Addison and Steele's successes in the periodical form were not so much the results of original genius as they were the perception of the possibility of amalgamating a series of techniques and tendencies predating the *Tatler* and *Spectator*. For example, Addison and Steele brought together the essay tradition (as practiced by Montaigne, Bacon, and Cornwallis), the Theophrastan character tradition of Hall, Earle, Stephens, and others, the how-to books of the earlier and later Renaissance, the desire to popularize the materials appearing in more learned journals—principally scientific ones—and a host of specific devices: the use of a single speaking voice (often termed the *eidolon*), the so-called club device, the division of subject matter (which Dunton had also anticipated), and, à la Dunton, the inclusion of letters from the audience.

In our own time these forms and devices have either disappeared or displaced into other areas. The *New Yorker*, for example, continues to present images of its guiding spirit, Eustace Tilley, and many gossip columns are written pseudonymously. Vestiges of the club device can be seen in the repeating characters of Mike Royko, and some of the

Are Addison and Steele Dead?

Theophrastan characters reappear as individuals in dialogue with Art Buchwald or William Raspberry. On the talk shows, individuals in the audience present themselves as characters—people presenting a pat or predictable point of view—because the nine-second sound bites available to them force them to sum up their vision of the world in a dozen or so words.

Essays of various kinds continue to appear, as do op-ed pieces. Popularization is more important than ever, as are how-to books. Letters to the editor are often the most interesting—sometimes the most frightening—elements in a periodical, and the multiple advice columns, covering such subjects as personal relationships, manners, gardening, chess, bridge, and household hints, continue to be extremely popular.

There are subtler displacements, for example, the glimmers of the character tradition in the portraits of erring spouses in the "Can This Marriage Be Saved?" segment of the *Ladies' Home Journal*; or the identification and division of subject matter in something like *Time* or *Newsweek*, which can be as potent an indicator of the state of culture in our time as it was in Addison's.

McCrea is concerned that Addison and Steele have disappeared because of their lucidity and clarity. (For that reason, of course, they are extremely popular with students when they *are* taught. The point did not escape Johnson's attention: "Whoever wishes to attain an English style, familiar but not coarse, and elegant but not ostentatious, must give his days and nights to the volumes of Addison" [*Life of Addison, Lives,* 2:150].) One can argue, however, that if one *does* permit them to disappear, one denies contemporary students the opportunity to understand a crucial aspect of their culture, one of both special significance in their private world (replete as it is with interactive videogames and other emerging entertainment technologies) and in their political world. What, for example, does the extension and amplification of the *vox populi* mean for our national political life—a more authentic democracy, an electronic raree-show, or a mixture of both?

There are other points that one might make. For example, Addison and Steele represented (re-presented, we would now say) English culture to a great many foreign readers. Their works are frequently found in American colonial libraries, for example, and when the young Scot James Boswell came to London in the 1760s, he continually searched for vestiges of and associations with the London of Mr. Spectator. In other words, English culture is often a construction of Addison and Steele's, and one need only look at the construction represented by the works of Hogarth to get a sense of each's selectivity. Mr. Spectator's London was the London in which many outsiders came to believe, and it is important to develop some sense of the extent to which the London of Mr. Spectator's creators might have been recognized by actual Londoners as a reasonably accurate representation of reality.

To allow Addison and Steele to speak unchallenged or, worse still, to die would be to fly in the face of some of the putatively key interests of modern criticism and scholarship. Thus, an approach to literary education that would exclude them would do a disservice both to "traditional" and "contemporary" modes of investigation and would deny modern readers an opportunity for insight into key aspects of their cultural and political lives.

The Addison and Steele example shows the dangers of an approach to literary study that is excessively based on texts; McCrea is correct in the fact that most modern students would not require the mediation of an English professor to help them understand a single *Tatler*, *Spectator*, or *Guardian* paper. However, such students most definitely would need the help of the Louis Wrights, the Walter Grahams, the Richmond Bonds, the Robert Haigs, and the Paul Hunters to place Addison and Steele's work in a context that is, ultimately, both interesting and important to them. In other words, the materials of "traditional" scholarship help make possible the activities of more contemporary scholarship and writing. One cannot attack Mr. Spectator's London as a construction that leaves out the lives and experiences of the majority of Londoners in the period 1709-13 unless one knows something about what Addison and Steele were attempting to do and something about the historical realities of the world that they selectively described.

What else have we sacrificed in our focus upon complex and difficult texts that require the mediation of the professor? McCrea looks back to Wimsatt and Beardsley's famous depiction of the so-called intentional fallacy and comments:

> Wimsatt never denies that authors have intentions or that works affect us emotionally. He rather argues that if criticism is to be a

field, a science, then those intentions and effects must be irrelevant. (*Addison and Steele*, p. 186)

That is the way that one keeps out the amateurs—by excluding two figures from the professional study of literature: the author (intentions) and the reader (effects). The author is excluded in several ways. For example, we have ruled out of consideration the author's moral, social, or personal purposes for writing his or her book. We have also excluded from discussions of literature treatments of the creative process per se. Current theoretical practices generally exacerbate this situation rather than ameliorate it.

I will discuss the position of the author in a later chapter. Here I would like briefly to look at the question of the creative process and to address it from the perspective of the bibliographer. Hershel Parker has argued that "for all their cosmic recklessness, the deconstructionists hold to the bland New Critical assurance that any text is complete and ready for their manipulations" (p. 233).

The comment comes from Parker's *Flawed Texts and Verbal Icons: Literary Authority in American Fiction*, a book that should be better known. Parker's point is that the "text," whose self-undermining the deconstructionist seeks to demonstrate, like the "text" whose image clusters, ironies, and ambiguities the new critic seeks to explore, is, naively, actually believed to *exist*. (One might take Harold Bloom's charge to heart: all formalisms share a great deal and ultimately lock arms against alternative approaches [Salusinszky, p. 54]). In the case of the former, for example, the boa deconstructor demonstrates conclusively to the teary-eyed logocentric historicist that a close and canny reading of the text reveals an echolalia of possible meanings rather than that single nugget of culturally hegemonic wisdom that the logocentricist had long ago written down in his commonplace book.

The bibliographer's point is that activities such as this rest on the naive assumption that the book is *there* (like the cow in Forster's *The Longest Journey*) and the games can thus begin. The book is *not* there in a number of important ways. The book is a construct, a cultural artifact, and endless debate over specifics always risks exposure later as so much wasted energy.

Anyone who has written an article or book knows that there is always some difference between the final, submitted draft and the published work. In some cases the differences are significant. Even in the "perfect" rendition of the final draft—no errors, no changes—the graphic representation of the text will have some bearing on its meaning. (Even a straight, photo-offset printing of the final typescript would carry a different implication than "absolute valuing of the author's intention." Quite the opposite, the printed text could appear to have been manufactured inexpensively, and this could imply a lack of commitment and seriousness on the part of the publisher.)

These changes can vary markedly. Hence the importance of the bibliographic study of the text(s). Literary history is littered with examples of grossly erroneous texts that were worried over by scholars and critics; many years ago Bruce Harkness gave some salient examples in the area of novelistic fiction: the overlooked fact of reversed chapters in *The Ambassadors*, scholarly ecstasy over Melville's "soiled" fish of the sea, which was actually "coiled," and so on. Some texts, of course, are "purer" than others, but unless and until the text in question is subjected to a full bibliographic examination, one cannot be certain. Still, the purity of a text is never absolute.

Any number of instructive examples might be offered. Parker, for instance, looks at Twain's *Pudd'nhead Wilson*, which the author was forced to revise radically in order to secure his publisher's approval. The nature of his revisions, however, mandated other changes in the novel, which he neglected to make. Thus, one must ask, what is (or where is) the text? Is it Twain's original novel in its final draft? Is it the revised novel, after Twain had made his changes? If so, the novel contains manifest errors. Is the novel then the revised novel, with the changes that *should* also have been made assumed to have *been* made? In other words, is it Twain's novel with additional changes made, platonically, in the mind of the reader, thus creating what "should have been," what Twain "should have done," what should, in effect, have fit the real "idea" of the novel in Twain's head?

These are not idle questions, and the more one knows about texts the more one realizes that the meanings (single, multiple, or potentially infinite) that critics find in texts are often—some would say always—contingent upon the actual facts of the texts' creation (and editing and revising and copyediting and correcting and printing in galleys and further correcting and printing in hard copy and reissuing and revising and reissuing, and so on). However, bibliographers often find it difficult to make their way into the discussion because the texts are many and their numbers are few. The economy of the profession as currently constructed permits the existence of very few such scholars; the principal ones can be numbered on two hands. Similarly, that same economy permits the existence of very few scholarly editors (these individuals are sometimes one and the same); a combination of temporal constraints, current interests, and the professional reward system makes it extremely difficult for the university to do what the university is, in many ways, designed to do: namely, protect long-term projects of basic scholarly research, in this case projects that help elucidate individual texts as well as the creative processes of those texts' authors.

Given the relative inattention that the profession devotes to the creative process, a number of gaps appear in what should ideally be a scholarly continuum. For example, in reading academic criticism, one often has the sense that critical strategies are based largely on the production of short lyrics. Spatial metaphors of the sort seen in New Criticism (well-wrought urns and the like) often still obtain. Our critical systems do not respond very effectively to texts that were extended works in progress, like Goethe's *Faust*. Nor do they generally look at the most basic kinds of problems and issues that confront writers. In the case of novels, for example, how do authors plan their narratives and how do they achieve such effects as pace? The novelist's challenge is to present an important idea, perspective, view, or concept, but to do it in eighty thousand to a hundred and twenty thousand or so words. (Poor boy searches for rich girl and finds America: *The Great Gatsby*. Who will inherit England?: *Howards End*.) How do they provide sufficient descriptive and narrative details—each and every one of them relevant to the central concept—without ever losing the reader's attention and while continually advancing the plot? How, in short, does the novelist deploy an idea, or set of ideas, that might be summarized in a single sentence or paragraph in a final manuscript of 350 to 500 pages? And how does one keep focused on the overarching idea (and keep all of the detail and superstructure complete and consistent) when one is at page 75, or page 200, or page 300 in the composition process?

Different writers do these things in different ways, of course. Some are notably successful, others less so. The former screenwriter and current novelist Robert Campbell makes use of computer technologies to construct time lines and keep elaborate and complex files on his characters. Some of the material is used; some is not; all of it is there to help Campbell to realize his characters more fully, whether his subject is the metaphoric sewers of Hollywood Boulevard in his Whistler novels or the very real sewers inspected by his Chicago ward heeler Jimmy Flannery in the softer-boiled series associated with that character.

The novelist James Ellroy, pioneering narrative techniques that faintly recall those of John Dos Passos but move light years beyond them, will begin the first section of a novel with seven to eight hundred pages of text and then boil it down to a hundred in a flood-of-consciousness style that has redefined the texture and intensified the impact of crime fiction narrative.

"True crime" writers have taken Truman Capote's "nonfiction novel" template and created a new form that is part history, part biography, part journalism, part docudrama, and part genre fiction, developing, in a single generation, a new form that occupies a significant portion of space in every serious bookshop. The amalgamation of historical fact with the narrative techniques usually associated with fiction, with the double requirement of both accuracy *and* interest, has generated a form whose development is extremely interesting to observe, particularly in such skillful examples as Sidney Kirkpatrick's *A Cast of Killers* or Joseph Wambaugh's *The Onion Field* or *The Blooding*. The point is that the processes of composition bear directly on their products, and the examination of those processes is always potentially fruitful, sometimes extremely fruitful. Bibliographers, editors, and biographers consider such issues in detail; critic-theorists seldom do.

Two very recent cases are instructive here: James Crumley's *The Mexican Tree Duck* and Charles Willeford's posthumously published novel, *The Shark-Infested Custard*. Each was among the most eagerly awaited of the 1993 summer's books. In a recent poll taken of professional mystery and crime writers, the consensus was that James Crumley is the reigning master of this particular branch of genre fiction. This is particularly noteworthy, since Crumley is largely unknown to the audience for mainstream American fiction. Because we are living in what Frank McConnell has called the second golden age of crime fiction, there are many serious competitors for Crumley's position.

However, *The Mexican Tree Duck* appeared some ten years after Crumley's prior novel, and the masterpiece upon which his reputation rests (*The Last Good Kiss*) was published some years prior to that. In the period between, Crumley was engaged in a number of screenwriting projects, but his novelistic audience was impatient to see the results of what they took to be ten years of labor. In the meantime he had issued two collections of essays, short fiction, and fugitive pieces, including work-in-progress material from *The Mexican Tree Duck*.

Inquiring minds want to know the extent to which Crumley had been blocked and/or the extent to which he was otherwise occupied, questions complicated by the prompt appearance of a new novel, *Bordersnakes*, in 1996. Because *The Mexican Tree Duck* returns to concerns about Vietnam (the subject of his ambitious mainstream novel, *One to Count Cadence*), brings back the protagonist of *The Last Good Kiss*, and pulls together the devices and tendencies of various forms of contemporary crime fiction, it is interesting to speculate whether *The Mexican Tree Duck* was a forceful summation of all that preceded it or a very nicely hedged bet. It may have been a bit of both. It is certainly a strong and engaging piece of genre fiction that will not disappoint. However, given Crumley's stature and the success—particularly among professionals—of his previous work, one would like to trace the growth of a crime novelist's mind and see the successive stages of composition of *The Mexican Tree Duck*. This is, essentially, a job for a skilled bibliographer/editor.

Willeford's novel—hyped as the book he considered his masterpiece—was actually written in the early 1970s as a four-part narrative. The first section originally appeared as a story, the second as a full-length, lush, pulpy novel (*Kiss Your Ass Goodbye*) in the 1980s. Given Willeford's stature (we will return to him in a later chapter) and the fact that his own experience as a writer spanned the generations in which the forms many of us now enjoy were all developing, it would be most interesting to know the details concerning the genesis of the book. Was it an unsellable favorite of the author's, mined as occasions arose? Was it complete but held in abeyance as Willeford enjoyed the success of the Hoke Moseley novels and the recognition associated with the film version of *Miami Blues*? Was it, in short, a trunk book or an object of its creator's affection that he was loath to release? Willeford's skill as a writer makes it difficult to jump to easy conclusions, and again, the skills and labors of a bibliographer/editor would help us to understand the work, thought, and method of composition of a notable and influential writer.

Our theoretical and critical systems should, in my judgment, do more than validate themselves while presenting a particular, limited perspective on selected types of literary material. Royal Gettman used to say that the English teacher's single, important task was to bring the student to books. In the current, "professionalized" ethos, that sounds more like the task of the grammar school librarian, but the fact that it sounds odd is, in part, an indication of how far we have diverged from what it is that we might do best. Gettman's thirty-year-old injunction, of course, is far more supportive of the desire to expand the canon than the practices of many modern professionals, for whom the "opening of the canon" is often merely a code phrase for the desire to substitute one point of view for another.

If the conditions contributing to the demise of Addison and Steele have involved a lack of concern with the author and the events and processes that precede the appearance of the artifact, what of the reader and the artifact's impact and results?

Murray Krieger, with many others, has commented on the essential importance of Kant to modern literary theory and criticism (*Words about Words about Words: Theory, Criticism, and the Literary Text*, p. 13). Kant's work cuts in a number of directions, a point to which I will return in chapter 5, but here I would like to note one thing concerning the *Critique of Judgment*. Kant's apparent argument for a special status for art, a status that frees art from judgments based on extra-aesthetic considerations, has been as problematic as it has been consequential.

This status sets art apart; it privileges it; it detaches it from more mundane concerns. It gives heart to artists and to aestheticians by signaling the special importance of art and noting the reasons for judging it purely on its own terms rather than on extra-aesthetic grounds.

Unfortunately, if Kant's argument is read in this unqualified fashion (as it often has been read), it does a number of other things. It offers the artist further justification for segregating himself or herself from society. It encourages a variety of formalisms that may or may not ultimately prove to be healthy for art. Put most simply, it provides the full justification for the separation of art from life. Hence Keats's comment to which Abrams has directed our attention, "I never wrote one single line of Poetry with the least Shadow of public thought," and Shelley's view that a poet is like a nightingale who sits in darkness and sings in order to add sweet sound to its personal solitude.

What Kant effectively does, it is argued, is rule out of order any questions based on extra-aesthetic concerns: Was the reader moved by this poem? Did the reader learn from this novel? Were the reader's sensitivities to the issues raised in this play deepened by this play? Did this sonata give the listener pleasure? Did this collection of essays make it easier for the reader to endure the burdens of his or her life?

If such questions are asked, they are not aesthetic questions. Art must not be judged on any terms but its own. It must be seen within its own created realm, judged by its own materials and its own sense of dimension, design, and coherence.

What this does, in effect, is overthrow the entire western tradition of art criticism, a tradition M. H. Abrams has described as *pragmatic* (*The Mirror and the Lamp: Romantic Theory and the Critical Tradition*, pp. 14–21). It nullifies Plato; it nullifies Aristotle; it nullifies Horace; it nullifies Sidney; it nullifies Johnson. It draws a line across the end of the eighteenth century and it states that from this point on all will change.

This would not be as damaging as it has been if students were still in firm possession of a historic sense, for they could see this type of aestheticism as a characteristic of certain post-Kantian activities, practices, and movements, an aestheticism that could be juxtaposed with earlier activities, practices, and movements, all of which enjoyed a far longer history and from which we can still profit. Indeed, as I will note later, they could look to the subtler form of pragmatism that engages Kant.

Unfortunately, some students see this aestheticism as settled reality, and the mediation of formalist English professors less taken with historicist and cultural studies approaches has further served to reinforce the illusion of its reality. Never mind the students' personal responses to art and their not infrequent preference for art that speaks to their personal concerns in extra-aesthetic ways. They can be trained to suppress such retro-tendencies.

Instead, they can take for granted a world of painting favoring abstract expressionism and look at something like the National Portrait Gallery's contemporary portrait competitions as strangely quaint. Once schooled in Mallarmé's dictum "After I found nothingness I found beauty," they can attend concerts of silent music and stare in rapture at blank canvases. They can assume to be appropriate and permanent practice an economy in which poets are largely ensconced in universities, where they are expected to train M.F.A. students who will then become university professors and write poetry for other university professors and other M.F.A. students. They can be properly shocked by Wallace Stevens's employment by an insurance company and even more shocked at the thought that such employment could have engaged his interests.

They can believe that writers—always, in general, countercultural—should also consciously separate themselves from their societies, living in varying degrees of alienation from those societies. Never mind the public practices and engagements of contemporary East European writers; never mind the practice of contemporary Latin American writers (all of whom, it should be noted, are every bit as cognizant of modern literary theory and its aestheticizing tendencies as their North American counterparts); forget such things as the resistance activities of many of the existentialists or the wartime code-breaking exploits of a number of American academics; forget, in short, all that partakes of that intellectual and artistic ethos that preceded the nineteenth century. (One could, for example, deconstruct the pronouncements of a tyrant in order to change the political order rather than deconstruct the writings of a sonneteer in order to secure a place on a conference room dais.)

An evolutionary attitude—the assumption, for example, that we finally got things right in the early nineteenth century and will now never turn back—is inimical to the humanities, which should both welcome the lessons of history and entertain the thought of great thinkers and writers within a continuous historical present. Our knowledge is neither cumulative nor sequential in the manner of the sciences. Thus, any arguments for the jettisoning of the past or of past ways should be examined closely. We *do* learn some things and some things are, more or less, settled, but we must be careful to distinguish arguments concerning such matters from arguments that can be little more than self-interested special pleading for the continuation of the status quo.

Pragmatic criticism, if one wishes to call it that, focuses precisely on the reader or listener, and critical practices that exclude or radically marginalize a consideration of the work of art's effects on the reader must be seen for what they are: conscious departures from the practices of several millennia that, in part, serve the economy of the literary professoriate and represent something of a professional conspiracy against the general public. Johnson's alleged comment to Miss Monckton, who was moved by the pathos of Sterne, "That is, because, dearest, you're a dunce" (*Life*, 4:109), sums up the attitude, Johnson, of course, later denying that he ever said it (even if he had thought it).

The generational, national, or international impact of a particular work (*Werther, Uncle Tom's Cabin, Clarissa*, for example) is, of course, a matter of great intellectual and cultural consequence, as the lovers of Rousseau (from Boswell to Marx to so many contemporary academics) should well know. The study of art's effects on its audience is of importance across the political spectrum, and its frequent banishment from academic discourse cannot be attributed to some form of progressivism. McCrea's book suggests that the banishment results instead from the foregrounding of the academic mediator. It is political only in the sense that it represents a desire for greater authority for one group rather than for another. This particular "political" action inhibits our study of our culture and ourselves, and it does so by muffling or silencing the citizens so that the guardians' voices might better be heard.

4

VATICIDE FOR FUN AND PROFIT

SEVERAL YEARS AGO, Sandra Gilbert was interviewed by Garrett Hongo and Catherine N. Parke for the *Missouri Review*. One particular comment among the many interesting ones she made stands out:

> I find a little disturbing and odd the kind of gulf that we have now between those who theorize about poetry in a way that gets the most attention in the academy and those who "just" write poetry. When I was at the School of Criticism, I remember one faculty member talking about how all history is a fiction and how we should celebrate "the death of the author." And I raised my hand and said, "Well, you know, I'm a poet and I know a lot of poets. And I just wonder if most of the poets that I know would agree with what you are saying." And he really said, before he thought about what he was saying, "But, of course, poets are not literary thinkers." (pp. 101–2)

Those who have followed recent trends in academic criticism know that the speaker probably would have said the same thing even if he *had* paused first and thought about it in detail. "Pen-envy," as Hartman has termed it, is not an uncommon phenomenon. Gilbert's interviewers followed her comment by suggesting that we are "in a decadent period—when criticism and creative work split and criticism itself fractures." Gilbert didn't disagree, though she suggested that feminist criticism, at least, attempts to unite different kinds of discourse.

Prior to the above quoted remarks in the interview, Gilbert noted the fact that up until the end of the 1940s and even into the 1950s, the major critical theorists were also poets. She mentions Tate, Ransom, and Blackmur and, before that, looks back to Sidney, Coleridge, Shelley, Arnold, and Eliot in England and Emerson and Poe in America. I would, of course, add some other names to that list, among them Dryden, Addison, and Johnson.

How can one actually say that "poets are not literary thinkers," given the undeniable facts of literary history? The answer, obviously, is that literary thought has been redefined. I mentioned earlier Crane's argument that pre-nineteenth-century literary writing is often concerned with what might be termed, in shorthand, rhetoric, while post-nineteenth-century literary writing tends to be more concerned with philosophic issues. There are many exceptions on either side of this particular divide, of course, but earlier literary criticism tended to concern itself with craft and effect, while later literary criticism, including our own, is more taken with such issues as meaning and signification.

This has been exacerbated by the introduction of the professorial mediator, whose mission it is, on McCrea's model, to ascertain meaning (or deny its possibility). The dyad of writer and reader has become a trinity of author, interpreter, and student, with what Johnson called the common reader often left out of the equation entirely.

In a piece on the "inevitability of Derrida," McCrea has suggested that the process we are seeing could easily have been predicted, his point being that we should think of criticism as part of an economy and that within that economy there is movement of capital. With the New Critics, the weight fell heavily upon the text rather than on the text's interpreter. The text was fetishized as an "autonomous verbal construct," a collection of verbal phenomena somehow imagined as constituting a physical object, "out there," separate from ourselves. Our job presumably was to note its beauties and complexities. Newer trends—no matter how radical or antinomian they may appear—are actually in large measure a reassertion of the authority of the critic/reader. The text is *not* separate from us. It is, in whole or in part, created by us. From the historical point of view, each of these positions represents a pole, with the emphasis swinging back and forth over time. Realistically, we all "know" that texts precede critics and also that those who read texts "create" them to some degree.

It would be helpful if more realistic descriptors were used, since critics do not create per se. The ink is already on the paper and the glue on the binding when they begin their work. They may so alter a text that it is no longer recognizable, but morphing is not the same as creating. Critics *filter* texts. Critics both narrow and expand the currently interesting range of readings that texts will support. Critics canonize texts that validate their method of reading, but "privileging" is not the same as creating, just as "shelving" is not the same as obliterating. Writers frequently change places within the evaluative consciousness of critics—Milton comes and goes, for example, depending on Eliot's current concerns and preoccupations; Bloom, so long absorbed with Blake, now turns to Pope, and so on—but while this pattern is extremely important, it is not really creative in any pure sense of the term.

The actual creative process, as I, following McCrea, have argued earlier, is now given very short shrift by academic critics, who see texts in quite different ways than writers. Poets are not "literary thinkers," remember. Academics presumably are, since those who do "literary thinking" in America write almost exclusively within an academic context. Their readership is not the general public but rather their normal audience: students, or a collection of similarly interested colleagues.

The fact that Johnson's common reader has been replaced by the student (or the colleague-as-student) is apparent in the fact that so much academic writing is so painfully convoluted and jargon-ridden, the unspoken assumption being that readers are part of a captive audience that cannot—as in the classroom—simply get up and walk away. The corollary is that academics often demonstrate their acuteness by presenting material that none but a select few can comprehend. They pride themselves on the fact that their audience is so small.

At first, this would appear to be a striking development, given the cultural background of contemporary students, who are used to manipulating a TV remote control and are unlikely to wade through the verbiage with which they are confronted. Their patience, however, may be compensated by the enormity of the statements offered, a trade-off for the language in which they are expressed. (One thinks of the famous Doonesbury cartoon in which the professor finally engages his students' interests by making statements that the reader realizes are outrageous and absurd but that the students consider striking and new.) At the same time, this academic model squares precisely with the practices of the information age, with literary scholars corresponding to narrowcasters or niche-magazine editors who fragment their audience into smaller and smaller cohorts. We are now on the brink of cable systems that will offer as many as five hundred different channels, but the Modern Language Association long ago made the change from meetings featuring large plenary sessions on large topics designed to attract large audiences to a multiplicity of small meetings of small groups dealing with small aspects of small subjects.

A parallel situation exists in periodical publication, a phenomenon known to librarians as "twigging," in which the tree of knowledge sprouts new limbs and then endless twigs. We move from a journal of English literature, to a journal of eighteenth-century English literature, to a journal of eighteenth-century English poetry, to a journal of eighteenth-century English rural poetry, to a journal of eighteenth-century English homespun rural poetry, to a journal concerned with the *oeuvre* of Stephen Duck, the thresher poet.

This, it is argued, is the result of specialization, and specialization is necessary for the growth of knowledge. This can be true, of course, though it is very important to continue to integrate the specialized knowledge into larger views of larger subjects. In reality, however, this kind of economy serves the professional needs of those who have helped to generate it. It creates opportunities by, in effect, reducing competition. In some cases it may open up new areas of inquiry and advance thought. In many, however, it simply creates white noise and drives readers and thinkers who seek to learn and not simply accumulate brownie points or curriculum vitae entries to the works of a few writers, to the publications of a limited number of presses, to the numbers of a small list of high-quality journals, and to professional meetings with a shorter list of speakers addressing important topics in longer, actually publishable papers. The white noise leads to a situation in which the integration of highly specialized knowledge into larger syntheses becomes far more difficult, and many simply abandon the attempt, opting instead for the creation of theoretical constructs or, in historical research, simply overlooking a portion of the scholarly literature and pressing on.

Thus, it is not uncommon to encounter theoretical work that overlooks the facts of history and historical work that repeats things that have long been known. Both sides then have their prejudices confirmed—on the one hand that unanchored theory is an abomination, on the other that so-called historical research repeats the commonplace and has little new or interesting to offer. And both sides are right, particularly when they present poor work as representative work.

In both cases, the audiences are narrowed. Exotic theory written in a private language hopes to attract a fit audience, though their numbers will remain few. Tedious historical "research," even that written in accessible language, cannot hope to attract a wide scholarly audience unless it offers new information. Who, except for a dwindling number of acquisition librarians, will fork over sixty dollars for a book that restates what we have long known or adds such a small portion of new knowledge that that knowledge could have been encapsulated in a single scholarly article or note? The problem, of course, is that the very economy of the profession encourages behaviors that are, ultimately, self-destructive or, as we might say, self-marginalizing.

This is a situation that Samuel Johnson would have a great deal of difficulty comprehending. What writer, save the most masochistic, would seek a *small* audience? Johnson would have difficulty with the notion precisely because he had no experience with an academy of such size and scale that it was capable of devouring nearly all contemporary poets and poetry and the vast majority of literary commentators. (The dramatists have largely been spared [though they are few in number]. So have the novelists, by and large, and the journalistic reviewers.)

One might, in fact, disagree with the individual with whom Sandra Gilbert had to deal and argue that *academic* poets are indeed literary thinkers in the sense that the modern academic understands literary thought. Many write small, introspective pieces for a small audience of colleagues at other colleges and universities. Few work in large forms; few write for the general public; and most are tied in to the reward system (and hence the behaviors) of the academy rather than the reward system of the professional writer (which, for poets, has largely ceased to exist). Poetry, university press directors often say, sells only to members of the author's immediate family. One response of those university presses has been to create what are, to some extent, Boorstinian pseudoevents: poetry contests that attract, amid the dross, a volume or two that can then be published with sufficient fanfare to attract purchasers in sufficient numbers to offset production costs.

Why should Sandra Gilbert be so troubled by the comment regarding nonliterary poets? She is, after all, an extremely successful academic, one of the leading literary critics of her generation and one of the top four or five feminist scholars in America. She is troubled for a number of reasons. The first is that she herself is a poet. The second is that during her time at Cornell, she was in contact with a series of writers, not the least of whom was Thomas Pynchon.

One should note that it is relatively rare for an English department to include a significant number of writers. One or two is not uncommon, 20 percent is virtually unheard of. For years, for example, the University of New Hampshire was rare in the fact that it had numbers like the latter. It even included an award-winning writer of nonfiction prose. (The fact that a great number of our students aspire to spend their lives writing nonfiction prose does not weigh heavily in faculty recruitment decisions. I once suggested to a former departmental administrator that we should do more with nonfiction prose; the response I received was, "Do you mean *expository* writing?")

I would suggest, from a Johnsonian perspective, that Sandra Gilbert's attitude differs from that of many of her academic colleagues for one of the same reasons that she is such an influential literary scholar, namely the fact that she is a person with broad, real-world experience. In addition to her scholarly training and work as a poet (she teaches writing as well as literature), she worked as a guest editor for *Mademoiselle* magazine, a position once held by Sylvia Plath. She was married at the age of twenty and had children right away. She also accompanied her husband to Germany where he was stationed while serving in the Army. In her career she has spent significant amounts of time on both coasts, and she is not unfamiliar with the culture of the commercial press (having been, among other things, the recipient of the Woman of the Year award from *Ms.* magazine).

Experiences such as this do not, of course, guarantee acuity or success, but absence of experience guarantees a number of things, and in the context of the life experiences of the majority of contemporary academics, Sandra Gilbert is a person whose experiential breadth is comparatively rare. That experience both broadens and deepens the perspective that she brings to bear on literature, and while it is impossible to draw causal lines, it is also true that Sandra Gilbert often brings to her literary activities a good bit of common sense. She is thus able to change the way people see literature and the world without constraining her effectiveness by indulging in special pleading.

Despite Sandra Gilbert's comments to the contrary, there are a large number of individuals who are comfortable with the thought of critics supplanting poets. It has been argued on many occasions, for example, that the very practice of criticism is itself creative and capable of attracting equal or greater attention than the "literature" under analysis.

This is a complex issue. An initial, commonsensical response would be, "Agreed, but only the strong will survive." In other words, the critic who intends to make claims on our attention that will exceed the claims of the author and/or the text must be equal to the task. There are, for example, a number of critics we will automatically read regardless of their subject, and even when their subject is grand and imposing we come to their work expecting them to engulf it and absorb it, changing it forever as they affix their signature upon it. Their numbers, however, are not great, and it is fair to say that the second-rate and the dull should not apply, since a situation will always obtain with critics that is not unlike that which we encounter with writers. In any generation, period, or century there are a few authors and a few books that will, ultimately, endure. The same is true, *a fortiori*, with critics, and it is important for each to choose his or her proper métier.

Each reader has his or her own favorite strong critics. In reading them our interest is in how *they* will respond to the texts, rather than how they will fade into the darkness and permit the text to command the foreground. This is particularly true with regard to texts whose numbers and cultural importance are of more interest than their individual quality. In such a case the critic brings order to a complex, sometimes confusing situation and *imagines* or explains literary history *for us*. Thus, we enjoy Edmund Wilson's reflections (con) on mystery fiction or Jacques Barzun's (pro). We profit from Leslie Fiedler's reflections on American and European popular fiction, John Cawelti's categorization and exploration of "social melodrama," Jane Tompkins's views of western fiction, or Marsha Kinder's exploration of video games.

Such an approach is safer when the literary texts and writers under study are smaller than the commentator. Great critics can handle great writers and good critics can handle average or marginal writers, but the general adoption of a strong-critic model involving the supplanting of the text by the commentator is dangerous in a professional ethos that is extremely uneven, imitative, and risk-averse. The great majority of the membership of the Modern Language Association, for example, is probably best advised not to attempt to play the strong critic's role.

Vaticide for Fun and Profit

We should learn from Samuel Johnson, but think twice before attempting to imitate him. For the average person the best advice is not to attempt to play the sorcerer unless you are prepared to end up looking like Mickey Mouse. Instead, follow the practices of someone like R. S. Crane: utilize the materials, both historical and theoretical, that are most likely to help illuminate the text in question. Forget *a priori* methods; avoid procrustean beds. The text is primary, not the critic. Remember the virtue of humility. Make a contribution to culture and society by helping to elucidate texts that have endured and by introducing society to hitherto-overlooked texts that, perhaps, should endure.

There is a pedagogical side to this issue that is of considerable importance. It has sometimes been remarked that the students of the strong are often noticeably weaker than one might expect. Harold Bloom addresses this point in an interview with Imre Salusinszky:

> "The trouble with you, Harold," [de Man] would say with a smile, cupping my head in his hands, and looking at me with an affection that always made me want to weep, "is that you are crazy: you do not believe in the 'troot.' " I would look at him, shake my head sadly and say:
>
> "No, I do not believe in the 'troot' because there is no 'troot,' dear Paul.
>
> "There is no method: there is yourself, and you are highly idiosyncratic.
>
> "And you clone, my dear: I dislike what you do as a teacher, because your students are as alike as two peas in a pod."
>
> I've never had two students who really studied with me who resembled either me or one another in the slightest. All that a teacher can do is to help someone discover what his or her own personality is. If that is sentimental humanism, let it be sentimental humanism. If that is selfishness, if that is high capitalism, if that is mercantilism: I don't care.... I would call it telling the only truth that one can tell, which is a subjective, narrow, limited, personal truth. (Salusinszky, p. 67)

And what is the first name from Bloom's lips as he enumerates the greatest critics in the English language? Johnson.

> The strength of Johnson—who after all invented the phrase—and of Hazlitt is that they show us that there is no distinction between the uncommon and the common reader: to be a reader is to be uncommon. (Salusinszky, p. 58)

And Bloom is clearly right. With all of Johnson's learning and all of his common sense and all of his attention to detail, there is always the looming, omnivorous personality that turns everything into itself: toting up Shakespeare's strengths and weaknesses, reducing *Antony and Cleopatra* to an occasion for his own dismemberment of the unities; holding Dryden and Pope before his eyes, comparing and contrasting them, as he moves from metaphor to metaphor, enjoying his own powers, particularly the fact that he can do what he does without the slightest need to stretch himself; dandling Richardson on one knee, Fielding on the other, and then turning over Fielding for a spanking; eviscerating his contemporaries' darling Gray with the most powerful of weapons, common sense and hard fact; and, perhaps most interesting of all, reducing the author of the most influential poem in English to a set of marmoreal impressions.

Johnson takes Milton, the poet responsible for that which, with respect to performance, is, in his words, "the second, among the productions of the human mind" (*Life of Milton*, Lives, 1:170), and then slowly proceeds to dissect. He excoriates Milton for his religion, his politics, and his treatment of women. He says of *Paradise Lost* "that it comprises neither human actions nor human manners" (p. 181). Soon after comes the judgment that has resonated for generation after generation of students:

> The want of human interest is always felt. *Paradise Lost* is one of the books which the reader admires and lays down, and forgets to take up again. None ever wished it longer than it is. Its perusal is a duty rather than a pleasure. We read Milton for instruction, retire harassed and overburdened, and look elsewhere for recreation; we desert our master and seek for companions. (pp. 183–84)

Johnson gives great praise where great praise is due, demonstrating—on a variation of his own pivotal principle—how Milton renders the probable marvelous and the marvelous probable. At the same time he bludgeons Milton for such gaffes as the confusion of the natural world with the allegorical:

> That Sin and Death should have shown the way to hell might have been allowed; but they cannot facilitate the passage by building a bridge, because the difficulty of Satan's passage is described as real and sensible, and the bridge ought to be only figurative. (p. 186)

Vaticide for Fun and Profit

This is the kind of criticism in which Johnson particularly excels, a criticism grounded in a knowledge of genre and craft—the application of the writer's eye to a writer's problem. It coexists with the learning of the scholar and lexicographer and the common sense of the common reader.

And it is a delight to observe—Johnson encompassing all and giving back a deeper, richer version of himself. But we must return to Winters's comment on great criticism: "Perhaps the only critic in English who deserves that epithet is Samuel Johnson." Johnson can be our model in the sense that he can encourage and inspire us. He can exemplify practices and behaviors. The course of his education and experience can instruct us. However, as Bloom notes, reading—especially in the sense associated with Johnson—is the most elitist of activities. One must share the sorcerer's learning before attempting to exercise his power, and when our society is failing to impart the most basic of learning, when it is failing to empower its citizens to function within it, why should we be as concerned as we appear to be with the development of additional or pseudosorcerers?

A strong reading of Milton is wonderful, but first one must know who John Milton is. One must know Spenser and Cowley and the traditions of both Renaissance and religious epic. One must know what allegory is. What is an Anglican? What is a Presbyterian? What is the Manicheanism in which Milton's Satan believes or the Pelagianism that he sometimes recommends? There is preparation that must precede strong reading, and how much strong reading will there be in a society with tens of millions of people who are functionally illiterate? And what is the first responsibility of the teacher in a society that Johnson would measure in terms of its ability to make a decent provision for its poor?

While I share Bloom's respect for Johnson and his judgment that our students should discover their own uniqueness, I would add the obvious point that before we hasten to be too unique we first acquire the foundational materials from which that uniqueness can be developed. An official posture that smugly privileges critics over artists and artifacts has its dangers. What happens, for example, when that activity falls into the wrong hands? The question was answered over twenty years ago by Charles Willeford in his novel *The Burnt Orange Heresy* (1971).

Willeford is a fascinating individual whose work should be better known within the academy. In the course of his life he worked as a professional horse trainer, boxer, radio announcer, painter, and English teacher. He studied art in both France and Peru and served in the Third Army in World War II, receiving the Silver Star, Bronze Star, Purple Heart, and Luxembourg Croix de Guerre.

Prior to the war his Topanga Canyon family broke up, and his grandmother, a milliner with whom he later lived, became impoverished. Thus, Willeford bummed around the Southwest before joining the peacetime army, the single form of employment available to him, and these experiences were recounted in his superb autobiographies, *I Was Looking for a Street* and *Something about a Soldier*. Beginning as a pulp writer, he wrote for many years, eventually enjoying some commercial success with his Hoke Moseley novels, including *Miami Blues*, which was adapted for the screen. Earlier, his novel *Cockfighter* had been similarly adapted, with Willeford himself playing a role in the finished production.

The Burnt Orange Heresy, one of his most popular novels, is, literally, a sendup of the art novel, its subject also being the world of art and art criticism. Presenting itself as crime fiction, the principal "crime" is anything but the sort of thing one would expect in the genre.

The book concerns a critic named James Figueras, a fussy, academic prototype for the psychotic protagonist of *Miami Blues*, Junior Frenger. The novel begins with the delivery of the newly published *International Encyclopedia of Fine Arts* to Figueras's Palm Beach apartment. The ethos of Figueras's reaction and attitude will be immediately recognizable to anyone acquainted with academic criticism:

> Two articles were mine. And my name, James Figueras, was also referred to by other critics in three more articles. By quoting me, they gained authoritative support for their own opinions.
>
> In my limited visionary world . . . my name as an authority in this definitive encyclopedia means Success with an uppercase S. . . .
>
> Clive Bell claimed that art was "significant form." I have no quarrel with that, but he never carried his thesis out to its obvious

conclusion. It is the critic who makes the form(s) significant to the viewer! (p. 3)

Figueras establishes his reputation by becoming the world's expert on the art of one Jacques Debierue, the acknowledged father of nihilistic surrealism. Debierue, a former framer, established his own reputation on the strength of a single work, entitled *No. One*.

"Why didn't he use the French *Nombre une*?" Figueras is asked.

> No one really knows. The fact that he used the English *No. One* instead of *Nombre une* may or may not've influenced Samuel Beckett to write in French instead of English, as the literary critic Leon Mindlin has claimed. (p. 43)

No. One is actually an open, gilded frame hung on a gray plaster wall over a crack in the plaster. The nail and wire used to suspend the frame have been left exposed. No one knows whether or not Debierue found the crack and framed it or actually created the crack himself. When pressed on the meaning of all this, Figueras—good follower of the *Critique of Judgment* that he is—points out that every work of art is autotelic. When pressed further, he offers the most common judgment:

> The consensus, including the opinions of those who actually detested the picture, was an agreement that the crack represented the final and inevitable break between traditional academic art and the new art of the twentieth century. In other words, *No. One* ushered in what Harold Rosenberg has since called "the tradition of the new." (p. 47)

For years a member of *Les Amis de Debierue*, Figueras is approached by a Chicago lawyer named Cassidy who has secretly brought Debierue to the United States. Figueras's proposed mission is to steal one of Debierue's paintings for the collector. In the process, of course, he will have the opportunity to firmly establish himself as the owner of Jacques Debierue, since Debierue has not been seen or interviewed in years and Figueras's name—following their encounter—will be, forever after, inextricably linked with that of the master. Similarly, no one has seen any of Debierue's work; hence Cassidy's wish to distinguish his collection by obtaining a canvas that will be prized for its rarity.

Figueras finds Debierue in a small house in Florida near the Dixie Drive-in, an establishment that Debierue, Figueras learns, regularly frequents, his favorite movies being those of the Bowery Boys and Ma and Pa Kettle:

> "I like M. Huntz Hall. He is very droll. Last week there were the three pictures one night with the bourgeois couple and their new house, Papa and Mama Kettle. I like them very much, and also John Wayne." He shook his fingers as if he had burned them badly on a hot stove. "Oh ho! *He* is the tough guy, no?" (p. 92)

Debierue enjoys grape snow cones, off-brand TV dinners, and fresh frozen Minute Maid (*fresh* frozen, he always insists). On his coffee table is a copy of *Réalités*; on the wall of one of his rooms is a dime-store print in a cheap black frame of *Trail's End*, the picture of the tired Indian sitting on his even more tired horse. Debierue has apparently been unable to secure copies of the pictures of the poker-playing dogs.

Figueras eventually ditches Debierue and finds his studio—a room filled with empty canvases. Either Debierue is blocked or he has always been a complete fraud; we have no way of judging. Figueras steals a canvas and some paints and eventually creates a painting that he passes off as Debierue's, an orange and blue abstract, representing the declining sun of Debierue's later years surrounded by a border of lustrous blue. The burnt orange purposely suggests Florida. In its tacky literalism the design of the painting also suggests something like the creation of a license plate, a close parallel being the standard blue and orange California plate, which symbolizes blue waters and acres of orange groves.

Figueras has his painting and he has his interview. Unfortunately the woman accompanying him, Berenice Hollis (who plays midwestern *eiron* to Figueras's East Coast *alazon*), has a conscience as well as a supply of common sense, and Figueras decides to hit her over the head with a tire iron in order to silence her. In the process, as she attempts to protect her head with her hand, he takes off one of her fingers. For Berenice, honesty is more important than abstract art, particularly fabricated abstract art. That is why she must die; some worlds cannot be bridged. (One thinks of Wellek—in his monumental history of modern criticism—being scandalized by Johnson's comment that he would prefer a portrait of a dog he knew to all allegorical painting. Why

Vaticide for Fun and Profit

should he be so scandalized? Has he never had a dog he loved? Has he never been bored by mannered art? If you have to ask . . .)

A year later—*after* he is lionized by the art community and Debierue has died—Figueras takes the woman's finger from an old cigar box and turns himself in to the police. He can do this because he has reached the pinnacle of his profession and there is simply nothing else left for him to do.

The novel ends with Figueras going over his Debierue article in the encyclopedia that was delivered to him at the novel's outset:

> I read my article carefully. There were no errors in spelling, and no typographical errors. My name was spelled correctly at the end of the article. A short bibliography of the books and major critical articles on Debierue followed my by-line, set in 5 1/2-point agate boldface. There were no typos in the bibliography either. . . .
>
> I opened my desk drawer and took out my brass ruler. Taking my time, to make certain there would be no mistakes, I measured the column inches in the *Encyclopedia* to see how many inches had been allotted to Goya, El Greco, Piranesi, Michelangelo—and Debierue.
>
> Goya had nine and one-half inches. El Greco had twelve. Piranesi had eight. Michelangelo had fourteen. But Debierue had *sixteen column inches*! The old man, insofar as *space* was concerned, had topped the greatest artists of all time. (pp. 141–42)

Interspersed throughout the novel is an array of quite funny set-pieces on art and art critics, but what we principally come away with—besides an account of a person who forges the work of a person who doesn't *do* work—is the extent to which small worlds (here the world of art and of criticism) can be taken as real worlds, part of the point of Barth's *Giles Goat-Boy* and David Lodge's *Small World*, both of which deal with the ethos of the university.

The novel demonstrates the nature of the "professional" perspective: Debierue is great because of the number of column inches given to him by commentators and editors. Critics are great because of the extent to which they can associate themselves with artists, artists whose work they then supplant with their own. In this case Figueras takes the extra step of not only criticizing and analyzing Debierue's work but also creating the very work about which he is writing. Willeford is, of course, indirectly demonstrating the nature of the modern "critical" process: a supplanting of the artist by the art critic whose work is more creative than that of the artist himself, decidedly more creative in this case, since the artist is a pathetic old man with a taste for kitsch, midcult magazines, and trash food, whose productivity as an artist is nil. The one voice of sanity is that of Berenice, a high school teacher, who, for her pains, receives a pair of sharp blows to the head with a tire iron. So much for cooperation across the curriculum.

The Burnt Orange Heresy is remarkably prescient considering the fact that it first appeared over twenty years ago. Recently it was reissued in the Vintage series of crime classics, though every word of it is as suggestive today as it was a generation ago. The novel demonstrates the dangers both to art and to society that are posed by the mutually supporting arrogance and narrowness of this modern critic's posture. It is not a trap into which all need fall, but it is a trap into which many will fall if the institutional structures and dominant orientations of the profession encourage one to risk it.

5

THE TWO KANTS

W<small>ILLEFORD</small>'s B<small>ERENICE</small> H<small>OLLIS</small> is well schooled in the apparent lessons of Kant's *Critique of Judgment*. James Figueras informs her that "criticism begins with the structure, and often ends there, especially for those critics who believe that every work of art is autotelic. Autotelic. That means—"

> "I know what autotelic means [Berenice responds]. I studied literary criticism in college, and I've got a degree in English."
> "Okay. What does it mean?"
> "It means that a work of art is complete in itself."
> "Right! And what else does it mean, or imply?"
> "Just that. That the poem, or whatever, should be considered by itself, without reference to anything else." (p. 45)

I spoke above of the "apparent" lessons of the *Critique of Judgment*, since I believe that Kant's argument is ultimately more subtle than it is usually represented to be. In some ways there is a "double tradition" of Kant like the double tradition of Johnson once traced by Bertrand Bronson. In the case of Kant, there is the towering genius on the one hand and, on the other, the inexperienced, untraveled aesthetician whose favorite music was Prussian marches and whose favorite verse was that penned by Frederick the Great.

It is true that the *Critique of Judgment* has been seen as opening the door to a heavily formalist, aestheticized, nonreferential, nonpragmatic tradition, though many of Kant's eighteenth-century antecedents are forgotten in the process. Donald Crawford has demonstrated the extent to which this reading of the *Critique* has been accepted, a reading emphasizing "aesthetic form over or even to the exclusion of subject matter, ideas, and content" (p. 92).

A handy instance of this kind of reading can be found in Hazard Adams's headnote to the selection from the *Critique of Judgment* in his widely used anthology, *Critical Theory since Plato*:

> Aesthetic judgments . . . do not consider the object with respect to an outer purpose. . . .
> An object judged aesthetically cannot be judged in terms of an external purpose. . . .
> The canon of accuracy implied by the Platonic idea of imitation is thus irrelevant to aesthetic judgment. All neoclassical external canons of beauty are likewise of no value, for they posit an external standard or purpose. . . .
> In Kant's theorizing we can observe a shift from interest in the reader's subjectivity and his response to art toward concern with the internality of the work itself. (p. 377)

Though I am not a Kantian, my guess is that Kant would see earlier pragmatic theories as comparatively crude and would argue that he himself, while appearing to be retiring into aestheticism, is actually in search of a subtler pragmatism. As Crawford argues, he clearly seeks to achieve some connection between moral virtue and aesthetic sensitivity. Kant writes:

> Both [the beautiful and the sublime] . . . are purposive in reference to the moral feeling. The beautiful prepares us to love disinterestedly something, even nature itself; the sublime prepares us to esteem something highly even in opposition to our own (sensible) interest. (Crawford, p. 146)

Thus, when we speak of the excessive aestheticism traceable in part to Kant, we should probably write "Kant," just as we speak of "Boswell's Johnson" in contrast to the real article. At the same time, this tradition is so often associated with Kant that the association itself is now embedded in intellectual history. Thus, I use it as a provisional shorthand.

There is another Kant, however, or at least another position that can be inferred from Kant's thought. The *Critique of Judgment* appears to sever art from the pragmatic tradition dominating western criticism up to the end of the eighteenth century, arguing that one should not inquire as to whether or not one has been moved, taught, purged, or pleased by a work of art, but simply consider art upon its own terms, see it as it is defined within its own diegetic space. The *Critique of Pure Reason*, on the other hand, presents us with other possibilities.

Kant's argument is well known. Trying to rescue some degree of certainty from the ravages of Hume, Kant begins by examining the differences between analytical judgments (which illustrate) and synthetic judgments (which expand our knowledge). In analytical judgments, the predicate belongs to the subject ("all bodies are extended"), but in synthetic judgments, the predicate exists outside the sphere of the subject, though it is still connected with it ("man is happy"). Analytical judgments help us to order and clarify our knowledge while synthetic judgments actually enable us to expand it. Clearly we can get the predicates for synthetic judgments from experience, but (the big question) can we have synthetic judgments *a priori*?

Kant reasons that mathematical judgments are synthetical and that they are made *a priori*. He argues that natural science contains *a priori* synthetical judgments as principles (for every action there is an equal and opposite reaction) and that metaphysics is meant to contain synthetical knowledge *a priori* (the world must have a beginning). But the problem remains: how are these synthetical judgments *a priori possible*?

His conclusion is that while *matter* is given *a posteriori*, *form* must be prepared for in the mind *a priori*. From this he reasons to the existence of what he terms "Categories," which he describes as "pure concepts of the understanding" (*Critique of Pure Reason*, p. 61). These include quantity, quality, relation, and modality. They belong to the mind *a priori*. Through them we are able to understand.

A contemporary way of thinking about the "Categories" is that they are a sort of built-in software that comes with our mental equipment. They enable us to learn *within the terms* of that mental equipment. They are not the superstructure for external reality but rather the preexisting structures within our own minds that enable us to apprehend external reality upon our own terms.

Nature, for Kant, is not a thing by itself but rather what he terms a number of representations in our soul. We do not apprehend things as they are in themselves; we apprehend them upon our own terms.

> We have always to deal with our representations only; how things may be by themselves (without reference to the representations by which they affect us) is completely beyond the sphere of our knowledge. (*Critique of Pure Reason*, p. 155)

Completely beyond the sphere of our knowledge. Thus, Kantian epistemology has been described as a system in which men and women apprehend their world through a set of spectacles that they are powerless to remove. They see things and they are able to get by, but always within the confines of their own modes of perception. Thus, our knowledge of our world is irreducibly analogical. We do not exist within nature (as the Kantian Frye is fond of saying) but across from it, on the other side of an unbridgeable divide. Our explanations are what Plato called in the *Timaeus* "likely stories"; they are, in effect, useful fictions, enabling us to both imagine and understand experience.

What bearing does this have on literary practice and our current concerns? Returning for a moment to the *Critique of Judgment*, Kant's apparent argument there is of a piece with a number of tendencies and practices that have accelerated since the beginning of the nineteenth century. In structuring a system in which art can be detached from society, a system in which art should not, in fact, be judged in relation to society (but only in relation to itself), Kant puts the full force of his authority behind the recent tendency of artists to retreat into solipsism and separate themselves, along with their work, from their societies.

It is extremely important that students realize that this tendency *is* a recent one, that it is not part and parcel of the poet's behavior and experience, but rather a characteristic that dates from the late eighteenth century, a characteristic that runs counter to most previous history and tradition.

The etiology of this development is quite complex. Abrams saw the French Revolution as a pivotal event, carrying so many romantic hopes and then dashing them on the rocks of the Reign of Terror. Beginning in a feast of reason, the Revolution saw Lavoisier, the greatest scientist of his generation and greatest chemist of his century, sent to the guillotine. Turning on boundless hope for human progress, the Revolution saw Condorcet, author of a *Sketch for a Historical Picture of the Progress of the Human Mind*, fleeing in fear from Robespierre. Finally, the Revolution gave birth to something quite different from what was originally intended, Napoleon arguing that without Rousseau the Revolution would not have been possible and without the Revolution he would not have been possible. Suddenly we are in a time when it is not bliss to be alive.

Years ago Edmund Wilson traced a portion of this pattern to the work of Mallarmé and the symbolists, using a signature work of the nineteenth century (Villiers de l'Isle-Adam's "Axel") to demonstrate the short distance from the castle of Count Axel of Auersburg to our own ivory towers.

Frye has seen separation and angst as implicit in the romantic method of proceeding. While the eighteenth century considers that writing to be most valuable which depicts human experience and psychology in the most encompassing manner possible, the nineteenth century opts for the ineffable over the common. The eighteenth-century literary ethos is heavily populated and urban; its general focus is man in society, not man in relation to God, to nature, or to the individual self. The nineteenth-century ethos (especially when filtered through Wordsworth) is a rural landscape of isolated individuals. The eighteenth century seeks to understand those aspects of life and experience that cut across culture and bind us together in our humanity. The nineteenth century seeks to depict the private experience of the individual that can never be fully shared.

Hence, for Frye, the signature work of romanticism is Coleridge's *Rime of the Ancient Mariner*, in which a single individual has gone past the normal bounds of society into the symbolic wilderness of the sea and experienced something he can never fully communicate. His life is changed forever as a result of the experience, and he goes about disrupting weddings and buttonholing guests, endlessly telling his own life story.

The experience is hardly unique to romanticism. Boswell is, in many ways, its purest exemplar, thrusting himself into the lives of such individuals as Rousseau and Voltaire, convinced that there is nothing within the world of possibility that they would rather hear than an extended account of the personal life and experience of James Boswell.

I would argue that this particular tendency of romanticism is brilliant and dazzling when done expertly, though the risks of systematic separation and indulgence in private experience are high, both for the individual and for society. When accepted as a model, however, it turns into a form of decadence that is self-marginalizing in the extreme. Shelley's high romantic angst at the triumph of Life is one thing; the whining of the contemporary alienated because they are receiving insufficient public attention or federal funding is simply embarrassing.

The distinction between the real and the literary is drawn more clearly in the nineteenth century. Reading Johnson is, essentially, reading Johnson. Reading Shelley the poet is somewhat different from reading Shelley the man:

> In the clear golden prime of my youth's dawn,
> Upon the fairy isles of sunny lawn,
> Amid the enchanted mountains, and the caves
> Of divine sleep, and on the air-like waves
> Of wonder-level dream, whose tremulous floor
> Paved her light steps.... ("Epipsychidion," lines 192–97)
>
> Sir,
>   You [Godwin] tell me that I promised to give you £500 out of my income of the present year. Never, certainly. How is it possible that you should assert such a mistake? I might have said I could, or that I would if I thought it necessary. I might have been so foolish as to say this; but I must have been mad to have promised what you allege. (Shelley, p. 575)

It is clear that we are no longer on the fairy isles of sunny lawn.

It should be noted that this separation of the artist from society is no more than a single tendency within the rich legacy of romanticism, but it is one that has a special appeal for hermetic societies such as the modern academy. There are other tendencies and other ways of looking at the romantic ethos of separation and loss. One, for example, is Wordsworth's interest in the lives of the poor and the (literally) overlooked—such as the human figures reduced to landscape features in the paintings of the late eighteenth and early nineteenth centuries that have been studied so well by John Barrell. Crabbe—whose work depicting such individuals Johnson knew and commented on—was there before Wordsworth, of course, as was Goldsmith, and their tendency to see the potential importance of all human experience, including the daily experiences of common individuals, is a Johnsonian hallmark as well. Johnson was advancing the cause of biography two centuries before it flowered as a literary form, and he was advancing the cause of social history two centuries before it came to dominate historiography.

Perhaps the most powerful nineteenth-century portrayal of such individuals, apart from depictions within the plastic arts, is in Dickens, who adds suspense and sentiment to what is already inherently interesting. The study of the individual, usually but not necessarily the middle-class individual, is central to the early development of the novel and part of its continuing triumph over other forms. Suddenly, the experience of real people is of interest to readers—"real" as opposed to the aristocratic, whose experience, Johnson argues, is so distant from that of average people that in reading about them we might just as well be reading romance, with accounts of dwarfs and dragons, enchanters, necromancers, and heroes fighting for days in blood up to their waists.

What is of most use, Johnson argues, is of most value, and what is of most use is the story of an individual like ourselves, with lessons we can follow in our own lives. This abrupt departure from the literature of the nobility in the Renaissance is one of the most important characteristics of our own literature, a characteristic that is adaptable to the needs of the eighteenth as well as the nineteenth centuries and comes down to our own day. (One day when my colleagues and I were drafting questions for doctoral exams, one individual suggested a question eliciting a discussion of "people who work for a living" in Restoration drama. The question was extremely difficult. A comparable question on contemporary essay serials or [a generation later] the novel would have been quite simple. Middle-class writing in the Renaissance, as in Deloney, is kitsch; middle-class drama in the eighteenth century, as in Lillo, is high camp; in the novel—the surviving form par excellence—we engage with middle-class characters and themes with avidity.)

While Goldsmith, Crabbe, and Wordsworth wrote of the rural poor and Dickens of the urban poor, modern crime fiction deals with the experience of blue-collar criminals and the lone, alienated individuals who bring them to justice. The psychopaths and lowlifes Jim Thompson writes about have their more genial counterparts in the Runyonesque characters of Elmore Leonard, but both exist at the margins of society in the wilderness, a wilderness that can and usually does exist in the city as well as in the desert. The underground inhabitants of Thomas Pynchon's world have their crime-fiction equivalents in the dark novels of Andrew Vachss. In Thomas Harris's *Silence of the Lambs*, evil can be studied in the behavioral science unit at Quantico or tracked within the entomology section of the Smithsonian, but it is best found at the true edge of the earth, in a place like Belvedere, Ohio:

> Feathers rode on the thick brown water, curled feathers blown from the coops, carried on breaths of air that shivered the skin of the river.

> The houses on Fell Street, Fredrica Bimmel's street, were termed waterfront on the weathered realtors' signs because their backyards ended at a slough, a backwater of the Licking River in Belvedere, Ohio, a Rust Belt town of 112,000, east of Columbus.
> It was a shabby neighborhood of big, old houses. A few of them had been bought cheap by young couples and renovated with Sears Best enamel, making the rest of the houses look worse. The Bimmel house had not been renovated. (p. 281)

We are quite some distance from Sidney's Arcadia, but not that far from Johnson's world. Johnson would know why Fredrica Bimmel, a victim of a serial killer who skins his victims, resided on Fell Street, since he himself had recounted the activities of "the fell attorney prowl[ing] for prey" in *London: A Poem* (line 16).

Thus, while part of the nineteenth century's poetic and aesthetic program involves the withdrawal from society and can be used to countenance—in decadence—the retreat into unbridled narcissism, there are other alternatives offered by the period. Unfortunately, the modern academy has largely followed the former and has constructed a parallel structure, Axel's tower, if you will, from which the outside world has largely been excluded. Within the vocabulary of the literary academy, the outside world can be considered to include, among other things, the creative process of the writer, the response to literature of the common reader, the intellectual and cultural concerns of the general public, the views of the journalist, the true educational needs of the country, and the real practice of real politics, including active participation in the process at the national level.

I should, in passing, absolve our social science colleagues who have bridged the worlds of reflection and action far more effectively and far more readily than have the humanists. The claim that governance is inherently technocratic and that humanists simply no longer have a place in this complex realm is a dodge. Technocratic demands have not intimidated Havel and did not intimidate Vargas Llosa (*Dr.* Vargas Llosa, who holds a Ph.D. from the University of Madrid). Moreover, technocracy makes many things easier. Anyone who has studied Bunker Wright's accounts of the difficulties and challenges with which Matthew Prior had to deal as an eighteenth-century diplomatist (constantly being paid in tallies rather than in sterling, for example) will realize that it was not easier to conduct diplomacy then than it is now.

The Two Kants

I spoke earlier of the pre-nineteenth-century tradition of literary craft: a tradition in which criticism often consists of how-to books designed for writers or common readers rather than of limited communications in a professional language for other academic readers. It is a tradition that is especially preserved during the period of romanticism and postromantic decadence by the novel, a form designed for the common reader, dealing with the experience of the common reader, and created by writers whose ethos and economy is commercial rather than academic.

This tradition, which focuses on craft, does so within the constraints of genre. Thus, while very little verse is written now that is other than lyric and lecturers continue to instruct their students concerning the "breakdown of genre" in the nineteenth century, the tradition of genre writing is alive and well in popular culture—in the novel, of course, but as well in film, television programming, and popular music.

The challenge of the genre writer is essentially the challenge posed by Johnson: how to achieve both novelty and truth, how to do old things in fresh ways, how to find new vehicles for established insight and wisdom. This is the challenge that particularly bedevils novelists, screenwriters, production companies, and programming executives. In popular culture, then, we find the practice of the eighteenth century still thriving, going blissfully about its business and paying scant attention to the practice and commentary in the hermetic worlds of the academy and the arts community.

The bridge between the periods has been the novel, though film and the electronic media have provided a great deal of help in sustaining the tradition of craft. Thus Camille Paglia:

> The idea that the western tradition collapsed after World War One is one of the myopic little sulks of liberalism. I will argue that high culture made itself obsolete through modernism's neurotic nihilism and that popular culture is the great heir of the western past. Cinema is the supreme Apollonian genre, thing-making and thing-made, a machine of the gods. . . .
> There is neither decline nor disaster in the triumph of mass media, only a shift from word to image—in other words, a return to western culture's pre-Gutenberg, pre-Protestant pagan pictorialism. (*Sexual Personae: Art and Decadence from Nefertiti to Emily Dickinson*, pp. 31, 34)

The Two Kants

We will return to the media and to La Camille later. I have not yet answered the question of Kant's relevance to popular culture, genre writing, and the Johnsonian critical tradition. The answer is very simple. If all of our knowledge is indeed analogical and if our intellectual challenge is to construct stories that enable us to conjure with a reality we can never experience directly, does it make a great deal of difference which story we write and which story we then study? The argument of the *Critique of Pure Reason* might serve to reinforce the ethos of, for example, genre fiction and popular culture, an ethos in which artists continually strive to represent the language of their culture and the language of that culture's human players with a significant degree of specificity and contemporaneity. Such artists seek to represent in order to understand. They create many of the primary fictions through which we interpret experience because they focus upon aspects of that experience that are pressing at the particular moment of their creation.

If, for example, we wish to better understand the notion of revenge, we might study *Hamlet*, we might study films such as *Death Wish V* and *My Bodyguard*, or we might study Andrew Vachss's powerful debut novel, *Flood*. We might study any one of thousands of depictions of revenge. Each of these images or analogies could help us, in some way and to some degree, to understand something about our world, though some would obviously be of greater use than others. While *Hamlet* is a greater work than the other pieces mentioned, the prevalence (in Johnson's sense of the term) of certain revenge fictions is instructive as we seek to understand a historical moment. The large number of recent vigilante fictions, for example, tells us something about our current sense of the law and the law's effectiveness.

I spoke earlier of Kenneth Burke's notion of "literature as equipment for living." How can the genre writer help us in this regard? If, for example, we wish to evoke a sense of place and study the manner in which setting or place can be experienced and poetically represented, we have a number of choices. We can, for example, bury ourselves in the topographic poetry of the Renaissance, which continues across the eighteenth century, gains momentum in the nineteenth, and finds expression in such effective modern works as Yeats's "Wild Swans at Coole" or Lowell's "For the Union Dead." Alternatively we can study the contemporary representations of a given setting—Florida, let us say, in the novels of Charles Willeford (he moved there, he said, because he was a crime writer and that was where the crime was), the Matthew Hope novels of Ed McBain (Evan Hunter), or the amazingly inventive dark entertainments of Carl Hiassen. We can study the Louisiana of Tennessee Williams or the Louisiana of James Lee Burke; both are powerfully evoked, though in very different ways.

Which is the "best," the "most effective," the "most useful"? Can the question even be asked? The relativism that is today so common is a petard that will hoist very nicely. While it can be used to downgrade the phallologocentric and point up the arbitrary nature of so much literary valuation, it can be used as well to upgrade the popular, whose devaluation, it could be argued, is no less arbitrary than other academic dicta. The problem, often, is one of either spatial or temporal distance. The academy prefers the remote to the proximate. One is permitted to study Indonesian puppetry but not Edgar Bergen, Elizabethan chapbooks but not the drawings of Frank Miller, the comedy of a seventeenth-century jestbook but not that of Richard Pryor. The desire is to avoid the "common," that which, of course, Johnson would have seized upon first. There is more than a little aristocratic snobbery in the academic posture.

Indeed, one can argue that popular writing should command a greater share of our attention because of its cultural resonance. This is where many find their values and the filters of their experience. When we write or speak of some aspect of our lives that is of broad human concern, the examples that are most likely to come to mind in a public or student audience are examples drawn from popular culture. That is where the Kantian analogies or Platonic likely stories are most often to be found, and if we wish to do authentic "cultural studies," we must study the cultural artifacts in which values are embedded and attitudes inscribed.

A further -*ism* that has been enlisted on behalf of popular culture is postmodernism, certainly postmodernism as defined by Jameson, where one of its defining characteristics is the collapse of boundaries between high and popular art. In this respect, one might argue that the eighteenth-century writers were the first "postmoderns." They had not yet experienced "late" capitalism as described by Jameson, but they were certainly as eclectic as we are, certainly as self-conscious (if not more so), and certainly interested in effacing the border between high art and popular writing. That border is, in fact, the subject of some of the period's greatest works: *The Beggar's Opera, Tristram Shandy, Clarissa,* and nearly all of Hogarth and Swift, to list the most obvious examples.

There is a further comparison that can be drawn between the eighteenth century and our own period, and that concerns the level of skill in popular writing. A generation ago, Dwight Macdonald published his famous essay "Masscult and Midcult." The extent to which that essay is now seriously dated (it originally appeared in 1961) is indicative of our current situation.

Macdonald divides culture into three categories. The first is high culture—his bailiwick—rare and precious but, alas, always in such short supply. The second is mass culture or Masscult, which is irredeemably bad:

> Masscult is bad in a new way: it doesn't even have the theoretical possibility of being good. Up to the eighteenth century, bad art was of the same nature as good art, produced for the same audience, accepting the same standards. The difference was simply one of individual talent. But Masscult is something else. It is not just unsuccessful art. It is non-art. It is even anti-art. . . .
>
> Masscult offers its customers neither an emotional catharsis nor an aesthetic experience, for these demand effort. The production line grinds out a uniform product whose humble aim is not even entertainment, for this too implies life and hence effort, but merely distraction. It may be stimulating or narcotic, but it must be easy to assimilate. (pp. 4, 5)

Macdonald then cites Adorno's tidy Marxist interpretation of the phenomenon. We are so alienated by our work within the capitalist system that we can seek nothing in our spare time but distraction. Masscult thus relieves us of both boredom and effort.

More insidious than Masscult is Macdonald's third category, what he terms Midcult. With Masscult we know that we are dealing with trash. With Midcult, however, we are given trash that masquerades as high culture. It is a corruption of high culture that is able to pass itself off as the real thing. Included in this category are the Revised Standard Version of the Bible, the *Atlantic,* "Omnibus," and products such as

The Two Kants

The Old Man and the Sea, Our Town, MacLeish's *J.B.*, and Stephen Vincent Benét's *John Brown's Body.*

Macdonald's pomposity is often matched by his ignorance. For example, he praises jazz because of its "folk quality":

> And as the noble and the peasant understood each other better than either understood the bourgeois, so it seems significant that jazz is the only art form that appeals to both the intelligentsia and the common people. (p. 15n)

Lovely. Macdonald, of course, is part of the (noble) intelligentsia, operating with what he later calls "the good conscience one has when one is attacking from the Left" (p. 67n). Folk art—the one thing that seems to unite the intellectual left with the National Socialists—is highly valued. After all, it brings together the noble we with the peasant thou.

Rock music, however, is seen by Macdonald as utter trash and is described in terms that are completely undifferentiated. All of it is the same and all of it is equally horrendous. Where did it come from and where does it find its inspiration? Twelve-bar black blues? Perhaps it might also be thought of as folk art? Macdonald doesn't stop to inquire. And from when does he date the beginning of the end? The eighteenth century. And what is the cause? That most evil of events: the growth of the reading public.

Macdonald, like the Scriblerians, is essentially a snob, prepared to look after culture on behalf of the "common people," which in America, he oddly believes, can be neatly separated from the bourgeoisie. High culture is, for Macdonald, noble in the same ways in which it would be considered so by the likes of a Lord Chesterfield, ensconced in the Ranger's House in Greenwich Park, watching the world go by and thinking of the poor peasant rabble who once assembled on Blackheath Common, trying in vain to alter the political equation. Johnson knew the tribe. He had waited unsuccessfully to see Chesterfield in hopes that he might provide support for the dictionary project, a venture actually made possible by a group of booksellers from the bourgeoisie.

Macdonald's evidence for the sudden decline in all things culturally holy is the relative sales figures of *The Spectator* versus the lower figures for *The Rambler*, four decades later. "The new public, it would seem, had read *The Spectator* because there was nothing worse to read.

The Grub Street publishers hastened to fill the gap" (p. 18). Thus, high culture is driven out by low as the capitalists trample the noble world they inherited with their grubby, middle-class boots.

For Macdonald, not reading at all would presumably be preferable to reading trash; that way the number of "common people" could be kept stable and there would be less likelihood of their joining the accursed bourgeoisie.

One very real problem, of course, is that Macdonald's facts happen to be wrong. Roy Wiles has shown that our estimates of the *Rambler*'s circulation have been grossly underestimated because we have failed to include its very frequent reprintings in provincial newspapers. Similarly, his claim that all writing up to the eighteenth century was written for a common audience is ludicrous. Thomas Deloney wrote for a different audience than Lyly or Sidney, and Tottel's *Miscellany* found its way into different households than Thomas Tusser's *Hundreth Good Pointes of Husbandrie*. Similarly, masques were directed at a quite different audience than broadside ballads or the popular fiction of the sort studied and collected by Charles Mish. But that is not really the issue. The issue is whether or not the writer whose audience is the common reader should be permitted to exist or instead be summarily silenced, the argument being that the bad will invariably drive out the good and once the number of readers increases, the seeds of high culture will irrevocably fall among the stones and brambles.

The argument comes down to more than just a question of taste. The Macdonalds value high culture and will do anything to preserve it. Without great art we are nothing. There is, of course, another side to the issue; some would call it political, some would call it moral. The alternative position can be encapsulated in a simple question. Should literacy really be withheld in order to protect high culture? Should the common reader be denied "common" materials because such materials will eventually eclipse high culture in the intellectual marketplace?

A parallel case would be the modern snob's loathing of mass-produced clothing and furniture (indeed of mass-produced anything). We are used to hearing the phillipics concerning K-Mart quality and the princes and princesses of polyester who are drawn to it. In the eighteenth century, clothing and furniture were handmade, and the period produced some of the greatest decorative arts and material-culture artifacts in human history. However, should we expect the poor and the lower middle class to now dress in rags and sit on telephone company spools in order to perpetuate that tradition and, hence, protect those artifacts?

The reality, of course, is that the wealthy can still possess handmade clothes and furniture and the poor can possess something serviceable if less "tasteful." Very few Londoners in the eighteenth century owned the products of the craftsman's art. Far from dreaming of inlaid mahogany, one-third of these people lived below street level and had to struggle for such basics as air and light, an effort complicated by the fact that many windows had been bricked up by landlords anxious to evade paying the tax that the government levied upon them.

Johnson thought Wedgewood's work interesting, but he doubted it would endure because of its high price and fragility. He was wrong, of course. Now anyone with a few pounds can buy Wedgewood everywhere, and while pine and plastic are always a furniture option for the poor, it is not too great a jump to cherry and even walnut for those who wish to so invest their money. We do not need to keep people in shacks in order to sustain the existence of Blenheim Palace. Neither do we need to keep people illiterate in order to sustain Tom Stoppard or Thomas Pynchon.

I think of the eighteenth century in a different way. I believe that genre writing for a popular audience (including something like Jacobean revenge tragedy—*Hamlet*) need not be trash. While the eighteenth century lacks the peaks of some other periods, it offers a relatively high level of common-quality writing. Contrary to Macdonald's opinion, for example, one can pick up any one of dozens of eighteenth-century periodicals and find writing that is very close to the standard set by Addison and Steele. The same is true of theatrical writing where there are many Garricks and Murphys along with the Sheridans and Goldsmiths.

I further believe that we are again in a period akin to the eighteenth century. There are relatively few great writers producing a handful of enduring masterpieces/monuments, but a great many doing exceptionally good work within particular categories for a large popular audience.

The best-seller list is often stereotyped and demonized as the domain of the trash writer, but that characterization cannot be squared with the actual facts of the situation. At any one time the best-seller list does include some of the kinds of books that would make Macdonald cringe in horror (Danielle Steel, for example, or Jackie Collins). However, it includes many other things as well. Pynchon's recent *Vineland* appeared there. The Rod McKuens find their way onto the list, but so too has Philip Larkin. A considerable portion of the best-seller list consists of genre fiction that is of quite varied quality, from the awkward and surprisingly uninteresting work of writers like John Grisham and Scott Turow to the marvels of a Carl Hiassen or Thomas Harris.

There are a goodly number of serious mainstream fiction writers whose work one could hardly label trash. Many of them are women: Toni Morrison, Margaret Atwood, and Alice Walker, for example. Until his recent death we had a writer of the stature of Graham Greene, an individual whose work commanded the attention of many academics even as it reached a wide popular audience. Greene was a superb genre writer, *Brighton Rock* being one of the four or five greatest crime novels ever written. In addition, of course, Greene wrote for the screen, as did Faulkner, Hemingway, and so many other serious writers.

I think of a writer like Orwell in this category and, of course, H. G. Wells. There is a great range of writing between Herman Wouk and Henry James. The fact that one is not Dostoyevski does not mean that one must be Danielle Steel. To reduce writers to three categories à la Macdonald (nobles, pretenders, and blights on the earth) is not only arrogant and nasty, it is simply ahistorical. There have always been solid and serious writers who were not Tolstoy or Thomas Mann, George Eliot or Jane Austen; in our own time, with a readership sufficient to absorb fifty thousand books a year in the United States, there is a significant number of serious writers producing work of high quality. Many are working in specific genres; many are writing mainstream fiction. Some few are even writing drama and poetry. In part the problem is the many; journalists keep up with a good bit of this material, but academics often do not and their common defense mechanism is to dismiss it.

There are far too many of these writers to begin to attempt even the barest survey, but one or two might be mentioned. James Lee Burke, for example, a writer now associated with genre fiction, labored for years writing fiction about the working class and their struggles against the powerful. Burke's novel *The Lost Get-Back Boogie*, poorly titled but beautifully written, was nominated for the Pulitzer prize, and some would say, with Charles Willeford, that Burke's novel *To the Bright and Shining Sun* is better still. His recent crime novel, *In the Electric Mist with Confederate Dead*, is a moving, magic-realist romance, the strongest yet of his Dave Robicheaux novels, with the possible exception of the powerful *Heaven's Prisoners*.

After his initial success, Burke struggled for a decade without a hard-cover sale, *The Lost Get-Back Boogie* eventually being published by Louisiana State University Press. Now his work is available around the world. I regularly encounter even his regional writing, such as *Lay Down My Sword and Shield*, in London bookshops.

James Ellroy, whom I mentioned earlier, has recently completed a four-volume chronicle of the Los Angeles that so haunts his imagination and memory, his best work perhaps being *The Black Dahlia*, written in part as a tribute to the memory of his own mother, killed in an act of random violence not unlike the death of Elizabeth Short. Ellroy is a writer of vast energy and ambition, redefining the crime novel with each book and providing a history of Los Angeles that, in interesting ways, parallels the African American chronicle represented by the books of Walter Mosley, a young writer whose black father and Jewish mother produced a son with an extremely interesting perspective on the postwar Los Angeles his father found after his move from the violent ghettos of Houston.

Genre writers are particularly interested in contemporary phenomena and their faithful representation. This is one of the ways in which they attempt to offer their readers what Johnson termed novelty and truth. One might point, for example, to recent novels such as Mitchell Smith's devastating portrait of society within a maximum security prison, *Stone City*, or Richard Price's depiction in *Clockers* of the lives of crack dealers and those who pursue them.

Some are extremely prolific, others less so. There are highly skilled craftsmen such as Lawrence Block, author of over a hundred novels, though now known principally for his Matt Scudder series, or Robert Campbell, who, at one point, was maintaining four separate series characters. There are also writers such as Thomas Harris, who work at a glacial pace; Harris generally spends seven years on each novel. Each of his books has been a smash best-seller as well as a successful film, and only one, *Black Sunday*, can fairly be called a potboiler (though it is a clever and engaging potboiler).

The list is a long one. My point is that within a single segment of a single genre, one can today find serious and able writing appearing at the rate of a book each week or two, and that is in addition to the oceans of ink devoted to diversionary entertainment and formula fiction. The same pattern exists in film and in television programming. Amid the muck and the commonplace may be found not only the occasional jewel but a steady set of accomplished and engaging pieces, many of them genre pieces.

There is a political dimension to much of this writing. Carl Hiassen, for example, writes of the systematic destruction of the Florida environment, and for all of his humor, the pain is never far from the surface. The ending of his recent novel, *Strip Tease*, is, as one reviewer commented, worked out with dazzling finesse in order to underscore the point that such satisfying resolutions of painful problems will never occur outside of the pages of genre fiction. Sandra Scoppettone, writing for years pseudonymously as Jack Early, is a living exemplar of Keats's notion of negative capability. Having written for years in the hard-boiled argot of male storytellers, she now writes in her own name about a lesbian detective whose personal relationships are explored along with her caseload. Scoppettone depicts the lesbian experience in a direct but not intrusive way, thus extending the range of her reader's vision and sympathy while serving up classical detective fiction. Andrew Vachss, a New York attorney specializing in cases of sexual abuse, particularly the abuse of children, fights daytime battles in the courts and nighttime battles in his art. His work now encompasses playwrighting for the London stage, graphic (that is, not very funny "comic" book) presentation of short stories, and a series of successful novels.

Vachss is fighting child abusers in his art, just as Scoppettone is exploring the sexuality of contemporary lesbians and Hiassen is defending what is left of the Florida environment. Their work is not propagandistic; it stands on its own without strong thematic props and attracts readers who come to these writers for their narratives as much as for their ideas. Put simply, these writers are involved in their societies. In the case of Vachss (and his wife, as well), they are involved at

111
The Two Kants

some personal risk. When Walter Mosley's father served in the army, he realized a range of experience and options for black men that he had not previously imagined. He was suddenly free to make choices, and he made them. Now his son depicts the variegated experience with which the family was personally familiar. He does it so that we all might understand, but he also does it in a way that we all can enjoy.

These are a tiny handful of examples of the writing being done by novelists treating real-world issues for a broad, middle-class audience, writing that is done with considerable skill, produced for an audience who, it is hoped, will be affected as well as entertained. This is not a scene of woe; it is essentially the literary ethos of Samuel Johnson.

The writers of Johnson's century not only wrote for a real-world audience, they also participated directly in political debate. Swift busily wrote in defense of the Irish and in support of the Test Act. Pope assiduously attempted to undercut the political strength of Lord Hervey, while Gay and Fielding sketched the underworld analogies for Walpole's behaviors and strategies. Goldsmith attacked the enclosure movement, Burke the depredations of Warren Hastings, and Burns the hypocrisy of the religious establishment. Boswell lobbied Pitt for support for the Corsicans, while Johnson himself decried the debtors' prison system, undercut the wartime propaganda of the government, and attacked their colonialist policies, depicting what we usually term the Seven Years' War as a fight between highwaymen for the property of a traveler.

If their work is not immediately accessible to a modern audience, it is not because the subjects are inaccessible. The subjects—as the eighteenth century tends to depict them—are timeless: pretense, arrogance, the abuse of power, hypocrisy, inhumanity, greed, oppression, and pride. What are unfamiliar, often, are the genres in which the subjects are examined. Poetry and prose (and painting) are conceived in formal, but not formalist, terms. The great writers of the eighteenth century are category writers, just as the composers are, and this fact should not occasion sneering criticism. (The point has often been made that those who claim to dislike formula writing had best avoid the works of such figures as Bach, Haydn, and Mozart.) The writers are often in opposition to their governments and even their societies, but they are neither isolated from nor separated from those societies. When they adopt the pose of the lone voice of reason, crying out for truth and for justice, they do so that they might plunge the knife a little farther into the arguments of the tyrant and liar (tyrants and liars being found, of course, in opposition to governments as well as in the midst of them).

This is also the literary ethos of Samuel Johnson.

6

THE WAR BETWEEN THE STRAW MEN

In the red corner, on my left, wearing the corduroy jacket and open collar, the challenger: hailing from Germany via France, the Poststructuralist Monster; his task—to destroy all that is good, true, beautiful, white, male, Protestant, and logocentric; his dream—to dissolve all texts and all meaning in a universal solvent that is half antinomian play, half God-hating nihilism; his seconds—a team of uneasy feminists and multiculturalists, joining in a shaky alliance against a far more fearful and certainly more evil enemy.

In the blue corner, on my right, wearing the tweed jacket and brown wool tie, the champion: hailing from late Victorian England via the University Club reading room, the Establishment Troglodyte; his task—to demonstrate the supremacy of western culture and the importance of preserving a fixed canon of texts with fixed meanings, reflecting a fixed world in fixed ways, mediated by male fixtures, whose sole *raison d'être* is the rabid defense of their own phallologocentric hegemony.

It is clear that stereotypes such as these have helped to perpetuate the culture wars and raise fears or hopes in the hearts of many of the combatants. Superstitions are paraded, John Ellis has argued, so that they can then be gleefully exposed. The question is, do the bases for these stereotypes and superstitions actually exist in nature? More to the point, are these the most accurate and useful ways of thinking about alternative approaches to literary study?

In his Preface to the Dictionary, Johnson comments on the multiple meanings of words in a natural language:

> If of these [words] the whole power is not accurately delivered, it must be remembered that while our language is yet living, and vari-

able by the caprice of every one that speaks it, these words are hourly shifting their relations, and can no more be ascertained in a dictionary than a grove, in the agitation of a storm, can be accurately delineated from its picture in the water. (Greene, p. 316)

I do not cite this passage in an attempt to certify Johnson as a fully credentialed deconstructionist, but it should be perfectly clear that Johnson, at least, appreciates the fact that signification slides, that words do not signify purely, and that texts do not reflect nature or reality or anything else in acts of absolute mimeticism. When Johnson asks that texts reflect nature, he is asking that they plausibly represent human nature, or, as we would say, human psychology. That psychology can include a great deal of uncertainty, nuance, confusion, and ambiguity. In fact, the psychology that Johnson prefers is markedly more complex than the simplistic psychology assumed by neoclassic prescriptive critics who prefer their literary figures to literally stay in *character*. Their senators should be wise, their monarchs sober, their soldiers plainspoken and direct. Rymer, for example, has predictable problems with Iago, problems that Johnson does not share. As a soldier, Iago is expected to be forthright and straightforward. If he has a failing, it should be a tendency to brag. Iago, however, is cunning and duplicitous. He breaks what they (and we still) call the rules. Johnson ridicules Dennis and Voltaire for similar forms of narrowness:

> Dennis is offended, that Menenius, a senator of Rome, should play the buffoon; and Voltaire perhaps thinks decency violated when the Danish usurper is represented as a drunkard. But Shakespeare always makes nature predominate over accident.... He knew that Rome, like every other city, had men of all dispositions; and wanting a buffoon, he went into the senate-house for that which the senate-house would certainly have afforded him. He was inclined to shew an usurper and a murderer not only odious but despicable; he therefore added drunkenness to his other qualities, knowing that kings love wine like other men, and that wine exerts its natural power upon kings. ("Preface to Shakespeare," Yale *Works*, 7:65-66)

If there are such simpleminded literalists as suggested by my aforementioned stereotype, Johnson cannot be listed among their number. The very notion of fixedness (and, *a fortiori*, the defense and maintenance of that fixedness) is, to him, absurd:

The War Between the Straw Men

> Perhaps, if we speak with rigorous exactness, *no* human mind is in its right state. There is *no man* whose imagination does not sometimes predominate over his reason, who can regulate his attention wholly by his will, and whose ideas will come and go at his command. *No man* will be found in whose mind airy notions do not sometimes tyrannise, and force him to hope or fear beyond the limits of sober probability. (italics mine, *Rasselas*, Yale Works, 16:150)

For Johnson, the manner in which we construct the reality within which we live can be a sign of mental illness—certainly it is in the case of the astronomer in *Rasselas* who believes that he is capable of controlling the weather. But it can be thought of in many other ways. For example, certain ways of constructing reality are generational, as Johnson notes elsewhere in *Rasselas*. We see things differently and we take greater interest in some things than in others at different times of our lives. Hence, generation gaps and generational conflict will always be with us. Their effects can be ameliorated if one is aware of their etiology, but their continued existence is a certainty. The fact that the young and the old look in different directions and subscribe to resultant attitudes that are predictably different is, for Johnson, an easily observed phenomenon.

Our personal construction of reality is also potentially therapeutic. Johnson frequently advises his readers to utilize mental devices to construct reality in such a way as to alleviate pain and increase happiness: saving and later utilizing the imagery that one acquires as the result of travel; moving from isolation, loneliness, and solitude into the sensory press of the city's streets; contrasting one's current state with the state of others in an attempt to elucidate the degree of one's suffering; and so forth. Like Blake, with whom he shares so much, Johnson realizes the extent to which perception shapes reality and experience and the extent to which the nature of our perception is within our own control.

It can be shown, I believe, that many signature attitudes of contemporary theory are anticipated in Johnson's writings, but it can also be argued that the thrust of poststructuralist theory is far more radical than anything envisioned by Samuel Johnson, so much more radical, in fact, that my stereotype depicted at the outset of this chapter is not really very remote from reality. Johnson may have been interested in mental illness and Johnson may have been interested in artificial hierarchies and self-interested political and cultural hegemony (which he treats at length, for example, in his review of Soame Jenyns), but Johnson, indeed, was no Foucault—but that is not my point.

My point is that the culture wars have been perpetuated in part by the construction of straw men who can be thrashed in print in the interest of stimulating the career development of the thrashers. The fact that the thrashing has been accompanied by what appear to be high emotions is traceable in part to the fact that the activity is so divorced from actual experience. If the realities were as bad as they are actually represented, there would be great cause for anger and alarm, but since the representations are such obvious exaggerations, the heat of the debate is mannered and artificially induced. This heat may not always bring light, but it attracts a crowd in a cold economy. It also keeps the emotions stirred for action, rather like the stimulation applied to and by the Red Guards when the revolution was flagging. The delivery of mail and scheduling of trains—like the slow sifting of historical evidence or tedious identification of textual variants—are far less engaging than the storming of battlements.

Let me give an obvious example. It is sometimes suggested that Derrida's ultimate quarry is God and that while the sliding of a signifier here and there might be perturbing, it is nothing compared to the prospect of a hollow universe. (Barthes commented that "to refuse to fix meaning is, in the end, to refuse God and his hypostases—reason, science, law" [p. 225].) Hence the alleged demonizing of Derrida by the God-fearing establishment, his defense by his enlightened followers, and a characterization of the debate that implies the heavy raising of stakes.

The world is not this simple. Heidegger, for example, is easily demonized after his experience with National Socialism, and it has been said, by George Steiner, that his shadow falls across the twentieth century—an ominous image suggesting the dark colors and stark-angled designs of an intertitle in a wartime newsreel. Derrida is much concerned with Heidegger, so we have more than the beginnings of a dangerous conspiracy, ripe for investigation and exposure, particularly when we look back to the God-is-dead grandfather within this group: Nietzsche.

George Steiner has also pointed out, however, Heidegger's enormous influence on twentieth-century theology, both Catholic and Protestant. Thus, only the studiedly simpleminded ideologue would see some evil progression from Nietzsche to Heidegger to Derrida (indicting the godless trinity) while overlooking such key developments in intellectual history as Heidegger's important influence on such figures as Rahner and Bultmann.

Assuming for the sake of argument that there is, in nature, some phallologocentric view of reality that can be described and delineated in detail and associated with concrete individuals, I would assume that belief in God probably plays some part in it. What is more logocentric than the Johannine gospel? The dismantling of this belief should then be a cause for concern. But is it? Is there some pietistic basis to the demonizing of Derrida that can be linked with the literary and intellectual establishment?

Again, I revert to my own experience, which, I believe, is here instructive. I attended the University of Notre Dame during the period 1959–63. The establishment there was not white Anglo-Saxon Protestant, but it was surely conservative. Dormitory lights were turned out at 11:00 P.M. from a master switch, and students were obliged to appear fully dressed for "morning checks" several mornings each week between 7:00 and 7:30 A.M., the purpose being to create the conditions that would lead to mass attendance of mass. When we read *Pamela* in our novel class, the president of the university was obliged to seek permission from church authorities to permit us to read a book that was, curiously, on the Catholic *Index*.

This was quite amusing to us. Copies were secured in a box behind the bookstore cash register and the checkout clerk was given a formal class list. No one was permitted to buy copies of the novel except those officially enrolled in the course. It was clear that the clerk had never heard of the *Index Librorum Prohibitorum* and had no idea why anyone would want to create disincentives for purchasing books, but she enforced the rules faithfully. The fact that copies of *Pamela* had long been available on the Norton shelf in the bookstore anyway did not escape our attention, but it must have escaped someone's.

This was a God-fearing crew. This was a religious institution. This was an institution with a conservative curriculum. The entire freshman and sophomore years in the college had a fixed curriculum, and courses in philosophy and theology were required in the junior and senior years as well as in the freshman and sophomore years. The faculty was overwhelmingly male; the undergraduate student body was exclusively male. Women were not permitted on campus after 9:00 P.M. except to walk to and from the bus stop and the student center. Women were not permitted in dorm rooms except during a brief period of several hours' duration on those Saturdays in the fall with home football games. During that period, doors had to be kept open at all times.

I believe that the alleged conservatism of the stereotypically imagined establishment has been much exaggerated, but I also believe that few of the individuals lodging those charges have ever been exposed to a conservatism of the sort to which we were exposed. (For some, of course, conservatism means a qualified belief in logic and the sense that words bear some relationship to things in the real world.) At any rate, in the belly of the conservative beast, there was no knee-jerk fear of the ungodly. *Language, Truth, and Logic*, for example, was a standard text at Notre Dame. I remember seeing its familiar cover in the same way that I remember the omnipresent blue covers of the Irwin texts used in what was then called the Commerce School. A. J. Ayer was a no-bones-about-it atheist, but he was an important thinker and we studied him. We heard endlessly of Heidegger (and of Bultmann) in John Dunne's theology classes. My principal French teacher had written his dissertation on Gide, whom we read, and we were as taken with Sartre as Derrida once was.

Derrida, of course, was not yet on the radar screen. His "Structure, Sign and Play in the Discourse of the Human Sciences" talk at Johns Hopkins was several years away, but we *were* required to read a host of other writers who might be stereotypically demonized.

Moreover, while the institution was immensely conservative, the faculty was hardly monolithic. It was an international faculty, featuring some truly distinguished individuals, such as Eric Voegelin (who taught a course on gnosticism to undergraduates, some of whom had trouble pronouncing the word), and it was a faculty that involved individuals of a great many faiths (including some with interesting conversion patterns, for example Jewish to Episcopalian), and, yes, a faculty that was not monolithic in its sexual orientation. The campus was the home of the *Review of Politics*, a relatively distinguished journal, then publishing the works of such individuals as Christopher Dawson,

Friedrich Meinecke, Jean Danielou, Hans Morgenthau, Herbert Butterfield, Hans Kohn, Yves Simon, Hannah Arendt, Waldemar Gurian, Alfred Cobban, Peter Drucker, and John U. Nef.

Thus, while the academic world is vastly different now than it was in 1963 (especially different at Notre Dame), it was not, even in its most conservative expressions, monolithic, stereotypical, and simpleminded. One of our striking experiences at Notre Dame, for example, was exposure to a set of literary clubs and publications that were in active and aggressive competition with one another. What we *were* prepared for was a system of intellectual expression and discourse that was susceptible to politicization, personal nastiness, favoritism, patronage, and the development of individual schools of thought.

One feature of the academic life then that I particularly remember was an ongoing series of faculty debates on highly politicized issues (Fidel Castro: Savior or Dictator?). This kind of debate is particularly interesting in a more conservative environment because the battle lines can be drawn more deeply. The result was a continuing, public clash of faculty opinion on important issues so that the students could see points of view publicly exhibited and publicly tested, with faculty blood being drawn for a change rather than student. The bland ethos that Gerald Graff now laments was really not in evidence then, and the English department was aided immensely by different sorts of experience as well as different sorts of approaches. We were fortunate to have individuals like John Frederick and Ernest Sandeen who were active in writing and had been associated with the University of Iowa, just as we had theorists carrying the New Criticism torch as well as a goodly number of products of the University of Chicago. We had faculty who had attended Columbia with Kerouac and Ginsberg and were full of stories concerning them. *Howl*, incidentally, was a very big poem/book on campus, far bigger than anything by, for example, Matthew Arnold, whose work we largely avoided until graduate school.

I saw many things in college, many, happily, that no longer exist, but I did not see monolithic simplemindedness as the cornerstone of an established order that was ripe for revolution. The topography of the campus did, however, include a large fact of life: Vetville, the home of married graduate students who, we were very grateful, operated a pizza parlor that rescued the undergraduates from the outrages of the university dining hall. When I arrived at the University of Illinois in

1963, their Vetville also still stood, again the home of married graduate students.

We are fond of characterizing the English academy in the United States as split between the French Nietzscheans and the phallologocentrists. The trace of truth inherent in that distinction has, I would suggest, been grossly exaggerated, while other splits, pairs, and dichotomies have been largely forgotten.

Some are of far greater historic consequence, and one of those is the arrival of postwar G.I.'s on the American campus. From a nation in which a small percentage of Americans attended college we have become a nation in which a large (too large, some have said) percentage now attends college. The number of institutions has multiplied, yielding an array of open mouths that, for example, far exceeds the capacity of federal funding in the physical and biological sciences. The ready availability of federal funding once drove growth, but that growth cannot now be sustained without twisting most universities into uncomfortable and unfortunate positions. This is a far larger fact of life on most campuses than the influence of Derrida, but its effects on the humanities curiously receive less attention than he seems to receive.

Prior to the war, American higher education was largely private. Now it is largely public and the concentration of private institutions is chiefly confined to the eastern seaboard. High-quality private education is virtually impossible without vast amounts of private philanthropy, and even then it comes at a high tuition cost.

The political implications of this phenomenon are not my subjects here, nor are the qualitative differences in the varieties of education offered to our citizens, another highly political matter. It is striking but not surprising that each receives comparatively little attention from the professoriate. That is not surprising because all universities must recruit gifted faculty on a level playing field; that means that institutions must bend in order to attract those who are most in demand. Thus, the institutions are shaped in part by the market expectations of the prospective faculty member, who often looks at an institution in terms of its ability to recruit effectively (what will my teaching load and research support be?) rather than in terms of its mission, goals, or intellectual signature—institutional aspirations and characteristics that have often eroded under the pressures of the marketplace.

The War Between the Straw Men

That professoriate has itself undergone significant change. It is a fact, for example, that (compared with earlier generations) fewer and fewer college professors have undergone such basic and once-common experiences as military service. It is a fact that fewer and fewer college professors still in the classroom have been personally affected by the experience of the Second World War, in contrast, for example, to the numbers of European Jewish intellectuals who came to American universities to escape the horrors of the holocaust, individuals whose presence had a dramatic impact on American higher education and whose pasts tempered their theoretical knowledge with real-world experience of the most compelling and devastating kind.

Given the professionalization of the professoriate and the growing distance in time from World War II, combined with the lengthy time required to earn a doctorate and the costs of attending certain distinguished universities (in foregone income as well as tuition), it often appears that the professoriate is less populist now than it once was. Certainly one is struck by the fact that an increasing number of the members of the professoriate seem to have never held any other job (except for part-time employment during school) prior to their academic appointments.

Thus, if one were looking for instructive dichotomies, it might be useful to draw a distinction between faculty with some prior connection and ongoing relationship with the real world and faculty who have never really known any world but the academy. The distinctions in experience represented by those patterns certainly have intellectual consequences for what transpires in the classroom and in the pages of scholarly journals.

When I think of the most obvious senior figures in my field, I think of someone like Jim Clifford, who started as an engineer, then worked for a rubber company in Boston and then a railroad car manufacturer in Evansville, Indiana. Jim wrote *Experiments in Atomic Science for the Amateur* eleven years before he took his Ph.D. in English at Columbia. I think of Don Greene, trained in mathematics, a paratrooper who wrote accomplished short stories long before he became Jim Clifford's greatest student. Fredson Bowers, who died recently, was more than the world's greatest bibliographer. During the Second World War he headed a naval communications group charged with the task of breaking Japanese codes. As David Vander Meulen has recently noted,

Bowers supplemented his income as a Brown undergraduate by leading a small band in which he played saxophone and Hawaiian guitar. He published *The Dog Owner's Handbook* (1936) in addition to five dozen volumes of critical editions. His book on dogs was based on his experiences as a judge of show dogs who raised Irish wolfhounds. He was also a collector of stamps and automobiles and a newspaper reviewer—for twenty-seven years—of classical records. It should also be noted that his work spanned several periods and countries and was not confined to a narrow chronological period or a particular author or literary form.

Both Jacques Barzun and Robin Winks have produced sufficient material on genre fiction to qualify for named professorships in popular culture studies. At the same time, of course, Barzun has been a university administrator as well as an influential historian. Winks—a distinguished member of the history department at Yale—is often suggested as the secret author of a famous series of pseudonymously written detective stories as well as a student of the craft. This kind of ambidexterity and breadth of experience is increasingly rare within the professoriate. Quality is always rare, of course, but the academic reward system has served to discourage such activity and undervalue such experience.

As we attempt to characterize the professoriate, it is important to keep a time line in the back of our minds. Someone like Roger Kimball, for example, will lament the "tenured radicals" who now control the academy. Actually, those in real control are often of Korean War, not Vietnam War, vintage. The so-called tenured radicals, to the extent that they exist, are in the following generation. I say "to the extent that they exist" since Camille Paglia has challenged the radicalism of this group, distinguished them from her Vietnam-era brothers and sisters, and accused them of being academic yuppies and masquerading conformists. Assuming, for the sake of argument, the existence of some "tenured radicals," one must ask how these individuals secured positive votes from their senior colleagues. The aged and tenured, putative nonradicals who tenured the "tenured radicals" must themselves have been radical sympathizers, since they voted to give indefinite tenure to the "now-tenured radicals" and did it at a time when threats of litigation were far less common.

The War Between the Straw Men

Following Roger Kimball, let us assume that the tenured radicals exist and that they politicize the university because they find politics more interesting than literature or they believe that everything is political, so they lay on with a vengeance. Why were they tenured by the "establishment"? Because they lied and falsified their real interests and inclinations? Possibly, in some cases, but hardly universally. Why then? Because the "establishment" agreed with them and were themselves tenured radicals? Possibly, in some cases, but hardly universally. Perhaps because certain approaches had run their course and the academy was ready for something fresh? That has, of course, often been suggested, but in that case the establishment would not consist of a group of hegemonic, simpleminded monsters trying desperately to hold on to power. *They* tenured the tenured radicals. Perhaps because they were simply weak? Possibly, in some cases, but weakness is not an intellectual position.

The reality is a complex one, but the vacuity of the stereotypes, whether coming from the right or the left, should be clear. We cannot accept a characterization of the profession that portrays the "establishment" as a gang of hegemonic, turf-guarding brutes and the rising generation as a band of anarchic madpersons. (One trip to one MLA meeting would dispel all fears. The anarchists are the ones with the knit ties.)

In lieu of such useless exaggerations, what other pairings or categories might be suggested? What other generational disjunctions exist apart from the purely political, granting for the moment that all things need not be political? Consider Frank Lentricchia's memory:

> My mother's father used to tell me, when I asked him what he did in Italy: "Shovel shit." He wasn't speaking in metaphor. They came here at the turn of the century, individually: my grandparents didn't meet—on either side—until they got here. To say that they were working people would be to say the obvious. My grand*mothers* were also working people. They worked in factories; they were not "ladies," or homemakers in the ladies' magazine sense of the word. My mother worked in a factory—for General Electric—for years: she was not a "lady." ... And I remember my mother showing me her hands. She worked on an assembly line, and she handled metal parts eight hours a day. She would say, "Look at these hands: they're a man's hands." And they were: heavily calloused, strong, rough. (Salusinszky, pp. 181–82)

I would not conclude from this that first-generation college students entering the professoriate from this period (Lentricchia was born sixteen months before me) would necessarily be politicized in a particular way or take a particular approach to literary study, but it is an obvious fact of life that those of us who came from blue-collar or gray-collar backgrounds, who completed college and graduate school with the help of scholarships and NDEA loans, have a markedly different view of the world than the previous generation's Harvard brahmins and Yale dollar-a-year men who came from (or married) wealth and privilege.

Kimball's tenured radicals are sometimes demonized as individuals who entered the academy because they scorned other possible occupations, but the opening of the doors of the American academy after the Second World War resulted in a generational difference that receives less attention than the establishment/radical stereotype, namely the entrance into the academic marketplace of first-generation college students who saw the professoriate as both an economic and social opportunity, a professoriate still populated by individuals with three or four names (and numbers following) for whom the professoriate has been far more respectable than trade and for whom the pre-Sputnik salary levels were largely an irrelevance.

I would not exaggerate the importance of this economic/social difference, but neither would I neglect it. For example, nearly all of my college classmates who have had successful academic careers came from working-class backgrounds—from New York garment district jobs to Midwest factory jobs. (I was the exception. My father was a first-generation college student, putting himself through night law school by doing scut work in a butcher's shop, but his death during my freshman year of college necessitated a series of scholarships and loans, comparable to those of my classmates.) My literary classmates and I were quite different politically, intellectually, and methodologically, but the two things we all had in common were the necessity to work for a living and the absence of names like Thurston Howell IV.

More to the point, our experiences were totally different from those of the Howells. I worked construction, for example, under Appalachian foremen with common-law wives and comparatively few teeth. I saw men fight on the construction site with such weapons as shovels and claw hammers. I worked for black foremen who, in a later time, would have owned the company or at least run it. A classmate of mine, now a distinguished academic, had a father who worked in a plant lined with heavy cement walls to mitigate the effects of the frequent explosions there.

I do not dredge this up to claim some sort of blue-collar chic. I do it to make the obvious point that individuals with different kinds of experience will bring different perspectives to bear on a number of the issues that now interest the English academy: race, gender, class, political theory, political activism, political and cultural hegemony, and so forth. The multiplication of first-generation college (and graduate) students in the wake of the G.I. bill and the expansion of the instructional and research establishment following Sputnik are important facts of academic life. To be sure, the "radical"/conservative dichotomy that has received so much attention deserves some portion of that attention, but the poor/rich dichotomy deserves some as well, and the two dichotomies are not necessarily parallel. Emotions have been heightened during the culture wars, for example, by the fact that a number of the "radicals" have also been rich and a number of the erstwhile spokespersons for the downtrodden have been largely innocent of the experience of the downtrodden. The spectacle of Brooks Brothers Marxists at elite colleges has rung hollow for many. A similar point is often made concerning upper-middle-class suburban feminists "speaking for" their poorer sisters, and Camille Paglia has raised the banner of the '60s generation, with its real wounds and bruises, its sacrificed ambitions and human detritus, against what she terms the academicians in the hour of the wolf.

This is related to the larger issue of experiential expectations. I believe that the thought of both Kant and Heidegger could have been enriched by greater experience in the outside world. I cannot see that it would be diminished by such experience. The same is true of those who study that thought. While it is true that intense personal experience can sometimes narrow our perspective or even blind us, I continue, with Johnson, to prefer it to innocence.

Each year, with the progressive hermeticization of the academy, we see fewer and fewer individuals with significant experience from the world beyond its walls. In part this is the result of historical circumstance, but in part it is also the result of conscious preference. We hire those precisely like ourselves more often than we realize. The dichotomy between those who have experience beyond the academy and those whose experience is confined to the academy is a fact of university life that receives far less attention than it should. It is also a fact with identifiable consequences.

There are other dichotomies as well, one, for example, to which writers as different as Alvin Kernan and Camille Paglia have called our attention, namely the difference between individuals with limited exposure to popular culture and those who grew up immersed in it. To illustrate the point I would suggest the example of the major American writer of our time, Thomas Pynchon. Pynchon's work effectively draws a line across the history of serious American narrative. That line results from Pynchon's deep experience of American and world popular culture.

Born in 1937, Pynchon would have vivid recollections of radio comedies and dramas, a culture whose imagery—like that of books on tape (a high-tech Victorian throwback)—must be created by the listener and speaker in tandem; at the same time he would have direct experience of the historic emergence of television, as well as that special moment in time when his family actually acquired its first television set. He would also have direct experience of the Hollywood studio system and the decline in the system's fortunes that paralleled the rise of television. The peak year of film attendance in America was 1946. The studio monopoly of theater ownership ended in 1947 with the Paramount decision. An imaginative individual who was ten years of age at that time would vividly remember weekly family trips to the movies as well as the emergence of television and the metamorphosis of radio.

On February 3, 1959, Buddy Holly, Ritchie Valens, and J. P. Richardson died in a postconcert plane crash outside of Clear Lake, Iowa. Don McLean called it the day the music died, but it was actually the day that demonstrated that the success of rock music was by then irreversible. The Beatles would later take their inspiration (and the source of their band's name) from Holly's band, the Crickets. Pynchon was in his early twenties.

It should also be remembered that those in Pynchon's generation who were exposed to early rock "concerts" were actually exposed to rock shows. "Acts" toured in groups and each played very short sets. The acts were extremely disparate; the only things they had in common were their roots in twelve-bar black blues and their ability to frighten parents, teachers, and clergymen. Within a given show, for example, one could hear acts as different as the Crickets, Jerry Lee Lewis, and black performers such as Sam Cooke or, at the other end of the spectrum, Little Richard or Screaming Jay Hawkins. Thus, the audiences in attendance were exposed to a wide array of styles, approaches, indeed a wide array of cultures, and that all in a brief period of several hours, with guards patrolling the aisles, ensuring that no one would attempt anything so rowdy as the act of simply standing up. Dancing, of course, was out of the question.

On the evenings of rock shows in Cincinnati, my high school teachers would load us with homework in the hopes of dissuading us from attending. One of my strangest memories from those times is a warning from my American history teacher, a balding cleric who drove a factory hot rod Oldsmobile with three carburetors and battened on the income from the Ohio sales tax stamps that he pressured his students to collect. He warned us that if we attended rock shows we were likely to be *embarrassed*, because it was "well known" that girls (they weren't yet women) were sexually *aroused* by such music and we might be *unlucky* enough to find ourselves in their company. To this day I am not sure whether he truly understood us or truly misunderstood us, but I have never harbored any doubt of the fact that he and many others immediately perceived, in some tangled way or another, the power that popular music possessed.

There is a developmental dimension here that is extremely important. It is not enough that you be alive when certain phenomena are occurring; you must also be at a stage in life where the phenomena can be of importance to you. The impact of early rock music is not nearly as great on those who were thirty-five in 1959 as on those who were sixteen.

For Pynchon, the confluences are nearly as perfect as they can be, and the manifest impact of popular culture on his thought and work is omnipresent. It is, in fact, so striking as to appear—to some readers—to represent a new form of narrative rather than an updated form of realism.

At the same time, however, Pynchon was classically trained at Cornell, studying science as well as literature and then working in the defense/aerospace industry as well as serving in the Navy. It is the intersection of classical liberal arts education with popular culture that is particularly noteworthy. Earlier generations were classically (conventionally, if you will) trained. Later generations—far more immersed in electronic culture than Pynchon's—have received a college experience that is quite different. In between, however, stands Lentricchia's generation, my generation, and we experienced both the full impact of modern popular culture and the still more-or-less intact impact of classical liberal arts education.

What this means is that there is a wide gulf between our generation (the early-mid senior professoriate) and those senior colleagues still many years from retirement and a nearly unbridgeable gulf separating all of us from the high-tech electronic generation that sits before us in our classrooms.

At a recent academic meeting, a group of us were discussing weekend plans; the age range of the group was approximately thirty-five to fifty-five. One individual commented that he was going to attend a Peter Gabriel concert. There was unanimous recognition of the identity of Peter Gabriel. I have no doubt that the slightest demographic tilt forward might have resulted in a series of blank stares. Similarly, I have no doubt that if one of us were to attempt to explain to colleagues a few years older *why* one should wish to attend such a concert, the cause might well prove to be a losing one.

In a nearby Georgetown shop there is an autograph store that markets signed manuscripts or simple autographs in elaborate frames with pictures of the signer and brass plates describing him or her (or them). It is kitschy in flavor but quite upscale in its prices. At the present moment there are autographs of Washington, Adams, Jefferson, Lincoln, the original astronauts, W. E. B. DuBois, Churchill, and FDR. There have been autographs there of Tudors and Plantagenets, of the boys of summer and the queens of nations. Among the most expensive current items is a signed photograph of Keith Richards in a frame that also contains one of Richards's guitars. The price is just under $20,000.

I have no doubt that a significant number of my older colleagues have no idea who Keith Richards is and would be totally nonplussed both at the asking price of the objects and the company within which Richards was to be found. If one pushed the matter further and pointed out that the guitar was a pre-CBS Fender and a collector's item that, in its own right, might bring $3,000 or more, the incomprehension could turn into stupefaction.

One could go through the entire shtick of the rock musician as latter-day romantic *poète maudit* and it would make precious little difference. The sheer weight and volume of popular culture is so overwhelming that it is far easier to simply avoid (and, hence, dismiss) it. However, those of us who have already been overwhelmed by it, who remember when the rhythm guitarist's name was Keith Richar*d*, whose consciousness is already filled with that culture's imagery, associations, and lore, cannot go back. Indeed, few of us would choose to. The same is true, *a fortiori*, of our students, whose immersion is far deeper.

Several years ago there was an article in a popular magazine by a very well known and very well positioned literary academic who was lamenting his students' knowledge of popular music. He noted that the students not only knew the full discography of their favorite artists but also what might be termed all of their recordings' principal textual variants. They knew the composition of the band's personnel at various points in the group's development. They knew who played what and who sang what on what cut of what album. The knew the changes and permutations. They knew the originals from the newly mixed. They knew the authentic from the bootleg. They knew the dates and occasions of the first use of specific instrumentation. They knew the melody and lyrics of unreleased songs, because they had access to concert tapes. The academic's reaction was that this was a terrible waste; these poor benighted individuals could have learned bibliography instead. The point, of course, is that they *had* learned bibliography, or at least discography. They had the skill. They had the patience. They had the technical knowledge of music and of the biographies and work habits of the artists. They had the physical materials. They had the knowledge of the industry that released the materials and an awareness of the identities, abilities, and styles of the technicians who produced them. They had a scholarly network of commentators with whom they interacted, and they had access to private collections as well as public repositories. And wherein lies the horror? They could have been studying the largely forgotten work of a minor Elizabethan dramatist rather than the works of contemporary artists. Why hadn't they done so, the print-culture academic wondered.

One might point to other dichotomies within the English professoriate besides those of the wealthy and the upwardly mobile poor, the experienced and the hothouse-raised, and those whose personal lives are developmentally pre- or post-broad popular culture. Instead of conceiving of ourselves as fusty humanists or avant garde theorists, for example, we could point to the rapidly growing division between the high tech and low tech. The first individual to prepare a Harvard English dissertation on a word processor is, in 1997, only forty-five years old. He is now involved in a project to extend and enlarge a server that will make the preponderance of the world's medievalia more easily accessible to colleagues through the Internet, a project that involves imagistic materials as well as verbal ones.

When I was in graduate school, there was a growing malaise among the musicologists that materials were becoming too easy to locate. Part of the training of the musicologist had involved the acquisition of the knowledge, lore, and wherewithal to *find* materials. Suddenly that grand old world was being eroded by the emergence of printed research tools. Now we stand at the brink of a vastly different situation—one in which a multiplicity of research materials can be made available virtually instantaneously.

Those who are incapable of using these tools will, to say the least, be at a serious disadvantage. There is already, however, a significant difference in point of view on the part of those who are technically adept and those who are not. O. B. Hardison's *Disappearing Through the Skylight: Culture and Technology in the Twentieth Century*, for example, illustrates how one can take many of the materials of modern thought (for example, the sense of separation from nature) and transmute them utterly through a high-tech perspective. Thus, where many romantic or decadent romantic discussions of the separation from nature are handwringing laments, Hardison's is fresh, open, and optimistic.

This dichotomy will widen at a pace that few can now even imagine. A little over a decade ago, laser printers cost $40,000, and no one on most university campuses had one except for the office of admissions, the development office, and the most lavishly funded of scientists. They are now readily available at a modest cost. In the late '70s it took a chip the size of a stick of Dentyne chewing gum to contain the memory held by an entire roomful of computers from the late '60s.

The War Between the Straw Men

What will be available in another ten years? Long-term pedagogic planning in the area of information technology is somewhere between difficult and impossible, because new hardware and software emerge so quickly and prices drop so precipitously.

It does appear clear that the next major development will involve a convergence of technologies in which such devices as televisions, computers, fax machines, and cellular phones will appear in single packages. The impact of such technologies will, of course, be enormous, but culturally the impact is a present reality.

Consider, for example, the classic Horatian notion of literature as a form of pleasant instruction. Many will keep these two facets in combination (teaching, pleasing). Johnson, for example, speaks of novelty and truth and requires the presence of both for literary effectiveness. Still others, however, will disaggregate the pleasure function, often because of suspicions concerning what might be "taught" or suspicions concerning what is *capable* of being "taught." Antiphallologocentrists and mimetiphobes will often seek to defer meaning, reduce it to a trace, or put it under erasure, choosing instead the dance at the edge of the abyss.

We hear much about the "ludic" element of literary production and literary study, but before we embrace it we should realize the full implications of the decision. As O. B. Hardison once commented:

> Deprived of a scenario, poststructuralism is left with a page on which it is impossible to write an incorrect sentence. This freedom can be used to expose contemporary illusions and hypocrisies. It can also become a kind of play in which nothing is serious. Recalling Nietzsche, Foucault calls it "the explosion of man's face in laughter, and the return of masks." This is probably valid, but its implications need to be faced. Where nothing is serious, Nothing (with a capital N) becomes the content of discourse. ("The De-meaning of Meaning," p. 404)

Moreover, if literature (and Rorty-esque philosophy) offers no more than what Schiller called the "free play" of art, literature must be prepared to compete with other forms of play. What percentage of the population is likely to choose the observation of sliding signifiers in Mallarmé over the forms of play that are now technically possible? Take the simplest of examples, something like the Back to the Future ride at Universal Studios. A hydraulically controlled vehicle (which never leaves its position) is rocked back and forth and tilted to simulate the sensation of violent time-travel. In the front of the vehicle is a screen upon which is projected a film that heightens the experience of the ride by constructing a narrative that involves such experiences as the vehicle's entering the jaws of an angry, ugly, and exceedingly hungry tyrannosaurus rex. The ride is comparable to Disney's Star Tours ride but with a significant exception: the Back to the Future ride's film is projected on an Imax screen, the multistoried screen on which many have seen such films as *To Fly* or *Blue Planet* at the National Air and Space Museum.

From one point of view, this is a four-minute plastic thrill designed to temporarily distract the exploited from their exploitation, but from another it is a fragment of contemporary popular-culture narrative. Where old-fashioned roller coaster rides force their patrons to wait in cattle chutes prior to a road-to-nowhere circular excursion over an open superstructure of steel or wood, Universal's Back to the Future ride moves its waiting patrons through a set of stations in what is imagined to be a scientific research building. At each station, footage is shown on monitors and the narrative is advanced. The story itself (of which the patrons are suddenly made a part) deals with the theft of one of the time-travel vehicles (which is to be overtaken by the vehicle in which the patrons will eventually ride); the action is not completed until the actual "ride" portion of the ride is completed, the mission is accomplished, and the time-travel vehicle is vacated.

The characters in the narrative are drawn from the original film and are played by the original actors. Thus, the ride brings the audience into the ethos of the film itself in a realistic way. In some ways it is far more engaging than cruder interactive or pseudointeractive experiences such as those in which a selected group of participants from the audience suit up, act, and are videotaped, after which the snippets of videotape are cut into an original film so that the couple from Van Nuys and the painter from Poughkeepsie are suddenly arguing with Captain Kirk on the bridge of the starship *Enterprise*. In the Back to the Future ride, the entire audience participates, not just a select few. Moreover, the research building in which the ride is putatively housed includes offices for the scientists with self-reflexive nameplates; actual scientists are named along with fictional ones and individuals associated with the production of the film. Thus, intellectuals, fans, and buffs can play mind games as well as ride games as part of the experience.

Those who reduce literary study to a purely ludic activity must be prepared for such competition. Of course, the emerging competition will be far more interesting: virtual reality bodysuits in which one can undergo experiences that will be rated above the level of PG-13.

The resulting dichotomy between a generation nourished on print and a generation nourished on electronic imagery is so vast that those from either side of the divide can hardly begin to estimate it. We should remember C. S. Lewis's statement that the advent of machines is nothing less than "the greatest change in the history of Western Man" (final par.). MLA conventioneers congratulate themselves on their membership in the avant garde as they agonize over the possible canonicity of Lady Winchilsea's verse or the inscribing of gender in Renaissance masques; meanwhile, their future students are at home playing Mortal Kombat, watching Johnny Cage kill his victims with a bloody, decapitating uppercut or Kano punching through his opponent's chest, ripping out a still-beating heart.

I would suggest that the differences between my straw men—sketched at the outset of this discussion—are smaller than the differences between either of them and the Mortal Kombatants they will soon find in their classrooms. While professors talk about the "real" in opposition to the "ideological," their students are already dwelling in the pervasively unreal world of what Baudrillard calls "hyperreality."

I would further suggest that the pedagogic issues, the policy issues, and the cultural issues implicit in that generational split are far more important and far more compelling than many of the battles we have chosen to fabricate and then fight. Given the magnitude of the real issues, we would do well to seek common ground before we begin to confront them.

These future battles are likely to be difficult ones, but at least they will enjoy the virtue of being real. John M. Ellis has argued, interestingly, that the battle of the straw men has, in fact, promoted the cause of conservatism by elevating the conservative posture to a status it does not enjoy in reality, the purpose being, of course, to then attack it wholesale. The result is a professionally convenient symbiosis between conservatism and putative radicalism. At the same time, Ellis argues, deconstructive strategies, at bottom, are quite conservative themselves (*Against Deconstruction*, esp. ch. 7).

Rather than receiving something new, we are given the endless demonstration of the fatuity of the old. In my judgment, the closest parallel is the black and white world of professional wrestling, in which bloated egos play a game of bluster, traveling from forum to forum, carefully staying in character for their followers, and demonstrating their power and agility in a dramatic exercise with a predictable ending.

John Searle puts this more genteelly, arguing that it is a characteristic assumption of many literary theorists that "unless a distinction can be made rigorous and precise it isn't really a distinction at all." On the contrary, Searle argues,

> it is a condition of the adequacy of a precise theory of an indeterminate phenomenon that it should precisely characterize that phenomenon as indeterminate; and a distinction is no less a distinction for allowing for a family of related, marginal, diverging cases. ("The Word Turned Upside Down," p. 78)

This is similar to Eugene Goodheart's description of indeterminacy as "in part what spills over the boundaries of the text" (*The Skeptic Disposition in Contemporary Criticism*, p. 102). The conclusion is that the true state of sublunary nature (as Johnson called it) and sublunary nature's texts is such that both should be rendered in varying tones of gray rather than in stark, simple black and white. To assume that distinctions must be rigid in order to be genuine, Searle points out, is to become Derrida's prey, but those most likely to find themselves in such a position are simpleminded absolutists. Such individuals are in radically short supply, but this has not posed any great difficulty. When they are not at hand they are simply manufactured; clay pigeons are shattered in lieu of live ones.

7

QUO VADIS?

One of the obvious differences between classical or traditional culture and contemporary electronic culture is the extent to which materials are available in formats that permit the viewer or auditor to experience them repetitively. For centuries, print materials were the only materials to which the audience could return at will. Successful plays, of course, could be seen again and again and printed copies purchased, but the live action could not be stopped and studied.

Original paintings could only be systematically reexperienced if they were owned by the viewer, and their price would make that impossible for most. Church and other forms of public art would be a notable exception, and such forms are especially worthy of study because of the fact that they also play a part in the rhythms and rituals of people's daily lives. More direct accessibility, however, would only be possible through the sale of prints and other mass-produced versions of original artwork. (Broad culture requires mass production and broad distribution. Hence, those who dislike mass production often exhibit a love of folk art; it minimizes any concern that without folk art the masses would not, in their system, receive culture at all. Authentic folk *art*, however, can generally only be purchased by the rich.)

Music, by and large, could not be repetitively experienced unless one owned and played a musical instrument. Music boxes—an exception, of course—could not contain long pieces. Church music—because of its place within the liturgical cycle—commands special attention, but it could not be repetitively experienced apart from that cycle.

Print materials, however, could be read again and again, and those of special, personal importance could be read constantly. The manner in which such materials are physically read and experienced deserves more attention than it has received. Paul Hunter, for example, has discussed the manner in which privately read novelistic narrative is recreated in the mind of the reader and in the *voice* of the reader—an experience that makes that type of writing far more personal than publicly recited forms. The fact that novels and other books are carried about like companions and displayed as both intellectual and domestic furniture is one of the reasons why more efficient methods of communication (printing and distributing volumes on microfiche, for example) have never displaced books. (See Hunter, "The Novel and the Contexts of Discourse," pp. 118–19, 138–39.)

Reading a novel aloud in a family circle changes the experience radically, a Victorian practice now replicated through the production of "books" on audio tape. Stores that market audio tapes exclusively are growing in number, and their products involve implicit theories of narrative. Some "books" are read by their authors, others by individual, professional readers. Which is most "faithful" to print narratives? How many readers of print narratives read—in their heads—in different voices? Do we simply recognize the different voices of different characters, or do we consciously strive to represent those differences in our heads? Should poets who seem to us bad readers record their own verse, or should that verse be recorded by "professionals"?

Questions have been raised concerning the gender of omniscient narrators. Do we automatically assume that a novel written by a woman has a female narrator, a novel written by a man a male narrator? Is this an idle question? Certainly a gender difference in a first-person narrator is significant. Is a book written by a woman falsified if it is read—on tape—by a male voice (or vice versa, for example Kathy Bates reading *The Silence of the Lambs*)?

Changes in technology bring with them accompanying questions that must be addressed, just as the physical presentation of different forms leads to different theoretical approaches. A poem can be seen whole on a printed page; thus, theories that tend to spatialize literary texts can be particularly useful in dealing with them. The existence of shaped poems, in the Renaissance and modern period, for example, further encourages this sort of practice.

Novels are more "personal" than many other forms. One can cheat and skip forward, reshaping the narrative by altering its putatively intended effects. Holding the book in our hands, we always know the distance from our reading point to the book's conclusion. Hence we can make assumptions concerning the shape of the plot and its likely outcome. We do not enjoy this advantage in the theatre, though the conventions of contemporary theatre (two-act, single-intermission structure, printed announcements concerning length, and the like) make it easier to make such assumptions. When the length of a play alters these assumptions dramatically, as in a very short play like *The Gin Game* or in an extremely short play like Arthur Miller's *Last Yankee*, the audience can become confused and respond hesitantly.

In the eighteenth century, unlike the twentieth, printed copies of London plays were commonly sold and read. Hence they could be repetitively experienced in the same way that novels and poems could be experienced. Particular works could take on ritualistic dimensions (*The London Merchant, The Beggar's Opera*) and become essential parts of contemporary culture.

In our own time, however, print materials have serious competition. Music is available on tapes and discs, as are plays, films, concerts, and operas. The materials through which these artifacts can be reexperienced are increasingly portable. They will soon become interactive. We can now freeze-frame film and manipulate sound. Electronic instrumentation that will reproduce the sound of any instrument in the orchestra has long been available at moderate prices. Soon we will be able to alter the imagery as well. For example, we will be able to watch a concert and select the musician whose playing we wish to observe in close-up. Since Christmas of 1993, one of the most popular of children's toys has been Mattel's *Story Maker*, an electronic book that enables the young reader to create a story by selecting elements from a list of options that are then combined electronically and played back when the narrative is completed. The possibility of repetitively experiencing those artifacts that are particularly enjoyable and/or meaningful means, of course, that certain forms of art can become intense, important parts of our lives.

Alienated literary commentators speak of "living in consciousness," abandoning the hopeless realm of American capitalism and plunging, like Spenser's Verdant, into a verbal bower of bliss. Frank Lentricchia, Terry Eagleton, and William E. Cain—among many others—have expressed concern that such activities as deconstruction represent conservative, even reactionary tendencies because of their implicit penchant for withdrawal and evasion. Eagleton criticizes the fetishizing of literature, the willingness to make it "the last place to play, the sole surviving antechamber of liberal hesitancy" (Eagleton, *Walter Benjamin, or Towards a Revolutionary Criticism*, p. 109).

Still, a life lived solely in consciousness has proven attractive to many. One problem, of course, is that the students of such individuals are not likely to follow them into *their* blissful bowers, since they themselves have been living in consciousness since the invention of lightweight earphones. The avant garde is actually at the wrong end of the learning curve. The younger generation (and a significant portion of the middle-aged generation) tuned out the adults, the traffic, and the doublespeak years ago.

Imagistic, repetitively experienced artifacts enjoy a number of advantages over literature in addition to the fact that they can be both more intense and more easily consumed. They can also, increasingly, displace some of the activities of scholarship. Laser discs of films, for example, frequently now include subsidiary material: alternative endings, unused footage, interviews with the director. One can purchase the theatrical release version of a film and the director's final cut of a film, thus viewing the artifact historically as well as aesthetically. The images are far sharper than those on videotape, and the costs of laser discs are more moderate and more stable. Many consumers are not aware that when they walk into a retail outlet, the images on the wall of television sets before them are often from a laser disc, thus leading the consumer to believe that he or she will enjoy that quality of sound and that degree of sharpness and detail when watching videotape, network, or cable images on one of those receivers. And, images on laser discs not only can be stopped and studied, they also can be located easily. A study group at the University of Southern California is actively involved in combining laser disc technology with computer technology so that, as we say, the text can be interrogated in sophisticated ways.

Each year we are shocked to hear the current statistics on the consumption of television programming. The numbers are uncertain, of course, since some people turn on the television set (and leave it on) the way others turn on an electric light. Still, such figures as the number of families with sets in service (98 percent), the number of hours of attention that they appear to command (seven and a half per day), and the number of violent acts observed by the average viewer prior to completion of grammar school (eight thousand murders and ten thousand additional acts of violence) are daunting. In a typical television season, it is estimated that the average adolescent will see fourteen thousand instances of sexual contact or innuendo in programs and ads. The one thing that is clear is the fact that imagistic media have replaced print materials. The process will accelerate rather than decelerate, and there is no turning back. As Kernan and others have argued, literature is dead.

But perhaps not quite. Print materials replaced oral poetry centuries ago, but oral poetry is still studied and still practiced. In fact, the replication of the experience of oral poetry, in, for example, rap music, is very much alive and well. Traditional poetry, sheltered and hence killed by the academy, has simply found a different medium of expression. Instead of the scop in the medieval mead hall reciting verse to the accompanying music of a stringed instrument, we now have poets playing fretted instruments (often before intoxicated audiences) in twenty-thousand-seat venues. The poetry is not always of a high order, but most poetry (and most criticism) has seldom been of a high order.

It is interesting to observe the manner in which the assumption of the poet's role in a nonpoetic age has been a conscious one. Jim Morrison, for example, explicitly detailed his poetic aspirations, and Exene Cervenka of the rock band X has published verse in print as well as sung it in concert halls. Even so obvious an iconographic cue as puffy-shirt costuming points to the rock musician's desire to look as well as play the part of the romantic poet. So many Chattertons, so little time.

The story is told of Kittredge's examining a nervous doctoral student and asking him how much of Chaucer he had read. "All of him, sir," the student replied. "And Shakespeare?" "All of him, sir." "And Spenser?" "All of him, sir." "And Milton?" "All of him, sir." "And Dickens?" "All of him, sir." "And Wordsworth?" Beads of sweat now forming: "Sir, I—I have not read . . . all . . . of him." Kittredge fired back instantly: "Neither have I; I couldn't be hired to."

Whether apocryphal or not, the story persists, for each of us has his or her own private Wordsworth (or a part of Wordsworth—the River Duddon sonnets?). Formal literary study imposes on students the obligation to read certain texts. However, cultural change as cataclysmic as that which we have undergone has made it increasingly difficult, if not impossible, to require texts today that were required a generation or two ago. Even the artificial resuscitation of the classroom cannot make some dinosaurs rise and dance. Certain texts will be avoided, even under the pressure of an impending doctoral examination, because they are simply too remote from our current experience, and certain texts will be put aside for the simple reason that new texts have crowded them out.

For example, can we realistically expect modern students to read something like Hooker's *Laws of Ecclesiastical Polity* in the same way that their forebears would have read it forty or fifty years ago? Can we really ask doctoral questions on Renaissance Barnabys like Barnabe Rich, Barnabe Barnes, and Barnabe Googe? Absent such knowledge, of course, students are incapable of constructing certain types of historical arguments, but historical arguments continue to be made in those areas that attract the interest of modern students, so that we can at least revisit the practice in the manner in which we revisit museums and archeological digs.

Several facts are simply overwhelming. The first is that none but a miniscule number of modern American undergraduate students possess foundational literary knowledge (Scripture, mythology, classical literature, languages). One cannot lecture on Barnabe Googe to a class that has never read More, Erasmus, Sidney, Ralegh, or Spenser, never mind the secondary figures in between. In the late 1970s, my then-department felt the need to institute a close reading course for those *graduate* students with undergraduate majors in English who had never seriously read or studied poetry.

Further, when one looks at the vast majority of contemporary academic works that involve the construction of historical arguments, the results are often so dispiriting as to make one question the current viability of the endeavor. The great literary historical scholarship of the postwar period has now often been replaced by works that recapitulate material that has long been known or by long (and expensive) books that add so little to our actual knowledge that they could have been reduced to a brief article or note. Important, unanswered questions remain, questions that require a sophisticated knowledge of literary history of those who would answer them, but where are the questioners and where is their audience? The point has been made that theory is so imitative and repetitious that one must advance absurdity (or at least employ exaggerated rhetoric) in order to attract an audience, like Blackmore's strain rising above the common din in the *Dunciad*. The same, unfortunately, can be said of historical research, where, for example, Camille Paglia (for all of her strengths) has indulged in rhetoric that has often resulted in her reduction to self-parody. (Paglia has expressed the desire to bring together Frazer and Freud. Apropos my remarks concerning the battle of straw men, it is interesting to note the tone and orientation of many of Frazer's comments with regard to the "savages" with which "we" seem to have so much in common. Where is one likely to find the hegemonic views of majority culture we must now so bravely strive to conquer? One place is in the writings of the 1890s.)

One area where one continues to see painstaking historical research is in the preparation of biographies, and it is gratifying to see fine work in this area (Andrew Hodges's biography of Alan Turing, John Mack's biography of T. E. Lawrence, Norman Sherry's biography of Graham Greene, or James Gleick's recent portrait of Richard Feynman, for example) receive critical recognition and reach a broad popular audience. The subject matter is not always as prepossessing as one might expect, but exceptional research and exceptional writing have resulted in material that has reached a wide, appreciative audience. As with true-crime writing, the techniques of fictional narrative have helped support biographical practice at a time when the blurring of the fact/fiction line is common. In James Gleick's biography of Feynman, for example, Gleick does an expert job of paralleling the work at Los Alamos with the slow process of making streptomycin broadly available. While Feynman and his physicist colleagues are breathlessly using the scientific method to construct a weapon of mass destruction, medicine—innocent or fearful of the scientific method—is moving too slowly to save the life of Feynman's tubercular wife, Arline.

Biographers, always practicing a blend of history and art, have learned to use the materials of each. Just as they broadened their own niche by attracting conventional fiction readers running in horror from art novels in search of books with a beginning, middle, and end and discernible characters, biographers now attract some of those whose taste for history and scholarship is not served as well as it once was by literary practitioners.

The pressures to alter traditional methods and the traditional canon also include what I would term the Leavis factor. I am thinking of the Leavis of *The Great Tradition*, announcing in the opening line of his first chapter the identities of the great English novelists. The nub of the issue as Leavis understands it is as follows:

> To be important historically is not, of course, to be necessarily one of the significant few. Fielding deserves the place of importance given him in the literary histories, but he hasn't the kind of classical distinction we are also invited to credit him with. He is important not because he leads to Mr. J. B. Priestley but because he leads to Jane Austen, to appreciate whose distinction is to feel that life isn't long enough to permit of one's giving much time to Fielding or any to Mr. Priestley. (pp. 11–12)

We cannot read everything and hence we should exclude the chaff and focus upon that which we consider to be the most distinguished. The principle was articulated in equally abrupt fashion by a college instructor of ours who began courses by inquiring as to the number of students in the class who had yet read *The Brothers Karamazov*. The tally was followed by the immediate injunction to the ignorant to read the book immediately, lest they suddenly die without having done so.

As the putative canon is enlarged and the use of secondary and non-print materials expanded, the ticking clock takes on far greater importance. Consider the use of imagistic materials in so-called cultural studies. The increasing array of literary commentators working in this area make frequent use of film, television narrative, and material-culture artifacts in their discussions. Film alone, however, is a very broad category. One of my Renaissance colleagues was once fond of lifting the *Short Title Catalogue* and saying, "This is *our* reading list." Students who wish to use film in their discussions must conjure with another list, a list that runs in the thousands of items.

Recently I was watching a John Woo film on laser disc. The interest in Woo's work—much of it enthusiastic if somewhat uninformed—continues to grow. In London, in the fall of 1993, for example, two Woo films (*The Killer* and *Hard Boiled*) were running simultaneously in separate Leicester Square cinemas. The disc included as part of its subsidiary material a cheater's guide to Hong Kong cinema: a brief survey of its history that was sufficiently detailed to enable the studious viewer to present himself or herself as an instant expert. The size of the industry is, of course, very large—more than enough to occupy the average academic over the course of his or her career. Woo's own output is also very large, and it includes a sizeable body of work in a number of forms that would be largely unfamiliar to a western audience. Similarly, the backgrounds of his actors in Hong Kong soaps (and the dialect of Chinese that they speak—with, as well, regional variations) divide the responses of western viewers from those of the filmmaker's Hong Kong viewers. In short, American students of popular culture looking at the variety of approaches to the action film may appear to be reasonably sophisticated if they are familiar with, say, a half-dozen of John Woo's films, but compared with an avid Hong Kong filmgoer, they know next to nothing.

But how is one to do less or do everything? To write of contemporary representations of heroism, to write of state-of-the-art versions of the action film, to write of the use of classical cinematic techniques (even old-fashioned techniques) in new ways is to write of John Woo. He cannot be overlooked. But, can one study him, authentically, without knowing the rest or even a representative sampling of his work? Can one speak of Woo without a reasonably broad understanding of Hong Kong cinema, of the extensive work, for example, of the Shaw brothers (with which Pynchon is familiar and to which he refers in his fiction)?

Something has to give. If one is serious about looking at new materials one must *look at new materials*. The pursuer of cultural studies who wishes to, as we say, engage with film, must engage with film. That means the film of the Americas and Europe as a bare beginning. Beyond that is the cinematic output of the rest of the world. The cinema of Hong Kong alone is enough to overwhelm the would-be investigator; beyond that lie, to give a single example, the awesome cinematic materials of India.

During my active duty military tour I spent some time at West Point, where I was stunned to learn that the library sometimes jettisoned materials when the growing volume of books reached the end of certain stack shelves. I was stunned all over again at the University of Wisconsin when I needed historical materials from the medical library and learned that materials there of a certain age were similarly jettisoned. Many of us grew up with the notion that libraries *contained books*; that was their *raison d'être*. They did not *provide access to information*; they contained books. At West Point, for example, I had immediate access to the holdings of the Ramapo-Catskill library system, which included the holdings of Columbia, Cornell, and the New York Public Library, but I was still bothered by the absence of those books that had formerly rested at the end of the shelf and had now been thrown away.

In some ways we are attracted by the symbolic dimensions of institutions. Libraries *contain* knowledge. Similarly, Bart Giamatti used to say that the very existence of universities was reassuring to people since their catalogues and physical plants provided the sense that there were places where one could go and receive answers to all possible questions. We know, of course, that this is not the case, but it is still pretty to think so.

We think of the classical canon in the same way. Its existence is very comforting. However, as Johnson pointed out with regard to Milton's depiction of Sin and Death, one should not move back and forth between the real and the symbolic without realizing that one is doing so. As scholars and teachers we work in a real world of real materials, and some of those materials must be taken off the active shelves if we are to have the time to look at new materials or at different kinds of already-existing materials.

There is no choice on this. The number of hours in the day and the number of years in each human life are painfully finite, and the number of texts we might read or view or hear grows day by day. Each generation, it might be argued—with Leavis and Eliot—revisits the tradition it inherits and sees that tradition from its own perspective. The texts, the issues, and the concerns that seized the attention of earlier readers are not necessarily those that seize ours, and while we require a certain degree of cultural literacy to participate in this long-term discussion, there comes a point at which we wish to read materials that, for us, are far more compelling than those that attracted our predecessors. This is not just the argument of contemporary Americans, growing up in a different place and time, concerned with new writers (or previously overlooked writers) and new issues; it is the argument of Samuel Johnson.

Johnson disagreed significantly with the literary ethos that he inherited. He thought Swift overrated and Pope simpleminded. He was not as taken with the novelty of Sterne as other readers were. He ridiculed much of Gray and preferred Dryden to Pope and Richardson to Fielding. He vigorously defended Addison. He disapproved of historiography that focused on kings, wars, and the acquisition of other people's lands to the exclusion of daily human concerns, daily human life, and positive steps in the amelioration of the human condition. Like many Enlightenment figures, he hoped for a historiographic focus that would pay far more attention to intellectual achievement and the extension of human capacity than political/military adventuring; the Enlightenment ideal is more like Boorstin's *Discoverers* (putting aside some of Boorstin's lapses) than it is like more traditional examples of historiography. He delighted in the materials of popular culture. Though he was a delicious satirist when he put his mind to it, it has also been argued that in the Age of Satire, Johnson was more of a satirist manqué. His basic human sympathies and his powerful capacity for empathy sometimes made him pull back before inflicting the death blow. He opposed governmental policy on several occasions, sometimes with a ferocity that resulted in censorship. He threatened potential attackers with physical violence when he thought it appropriate, and he was not averse to resorting to physical violence when more civil behaviors proved unsuccessful. He argued for social history two hundred years before its practice became widespread and made a very strong case for biography, a form that is just now in what might be considered its golden age. In the Preface to his edition of Shakespeare he scored the views of established theorists as well as the behavior of dryasdusts, whose petty battles he sought to explain. Although his cultural literacy and respect for classical writing and learning were clear and imposing, his practices as both a reader and a human being suggest great independence, a wide-ranging populism, and constant impatience with the status quo.

He shocked his friends by making his black manservant, Francis Barber, residuary legatee of his estate, upset his companions at Oxford with a toast to the next uprising of the slaves in the West Indies, and savaged the American slave owners for their own yelps for liberty. G. B. Hill surprised his contemporaries when he announced his intentions to write of Johnson's radicalism—something whose very existence they initially doubted—but we have long been familiar with it and with the fact that it coexists nicely with his practices as a reader, critic, and social and political commentator.

What would Johnson's position be with regard to our current situation in literary study? As I have already indicated, he would be extremely impatient with the study of theory for theory's sake, and he would be deeply suspicious of applications of theory that were largely innocent of experience. Remember—the ultimate claim to poetical honors, he tells us, must come from "the common sense of readers uncorrupted with literary prejudices," and "common sense and common honesty" are "names of greater authority than that of *Horace*." As to theory in general, he decries "the cant of those who judge by principles rather than perception" (Brown, p. 105).

He would also, the Preface to Shakespeare makes clear, be impatient with academic writing, but what *is* academic writing? It is not, exclusively, writing done by academics, some of whom write lucidly for a wide audience. It certainly can include writing that is done in some "popular" magazines. The unfortunate end point of specialization often seems to be an inability to communicate in clear language for a broadly educated popular audience. The reviews of contemporary music in *Rolling Stone*, for example, can be as recondite and exclusionary as the reviews in scholarly journals. University-based writers may be particularly susceptible to the malady, but the root causes of specialization and attempted professionalization can strike anyone.

Academics sometimes protest that their subject *is* technical and, hence, must be addressed in technical language. Up to a point, that is understandable. For example, if one looks at technical passages in magazines designed for members of a particular trade, one will find a comparable situation. An interview with a musician in, for example, *Guitar Player* that elicits information on the basic instrumentation and electronic enhancements on a particular album cut will yield responses that no one but a hardened professional will even begin to be able to comprehend.

Moreover, one should not bind academics to write in popular language when the discussion is clearly for a limited few. If one is talking about computer applications that one might employ in order to generate a short title catalogue or copy-text decisions that one must make in the design of a discrete editorial project, one should not be bound to speak in the language of the literary primer. The issues are technical and the intended audience small.

That is not the problem. The problem is *unnecessary* specialization and professionalization, particularly in a field that deals with so deeply human an endeavor as literature, which itself deals with such broad issues as love and hate, hope and memory, the individual and society, and dozens of others of equally high importance. The problem is the broad avoidance of clear language and large, important subjects for research; permitting the risk-averse individual to collapse into the professional self and dwell behind guildhall doors; perpetuating a reward system that privileges the narrow, protects the already fearful and conservative, and charts career paths and behaviors that involve the exclusion or marginalization of a host of literary activities, literary concerns, and literary issues.

When English departments are uncomfortable with all creative writers but those who are their own cultural and educational reflections, when they give short shrift to such phenomena as the creative process and the reactions of common readers to texts, when they are intolerant of any views but those enjoying contemporary currency, and when they systematically exclude nonacademic literary writers (including journalists) from their consideration, we have a problem. The problem is not with what is claimed to be radical subject matter, radical approaches, or the shocking of the pious and the established. The issues of current interest—the inscribing of gender; the manner in which what we mistakenly take to be reality has actually been culturally constructed; the embracing of diverse traditions, forms, and writers; the relationship between art and politics; the relationship between education and politics; the nature, extent, dimensions, and possible existence of *meaning*; the structure of mind, consciousness, the psyche, and the brain; the hegemonic possibilities of art and culture; and the periodization and description of the postmodern era—to name but a few—are issues of great interest and, potentially, of great importance.

The problem lies in the *manner* in which these issues are approached and, often, trivialized. That manner is, far too often, imitative, derivative, repetitious, ahistorical, crushingly boring, excessively narrow, and, above all, *safe*. The boredom is increased, as Terry Eagleton has argued, when the ongoing subject of discourse becomes (as it so often does) the impotence of that discourse (*Literary Theory: An Introduction*, p. 146). From time to time we all seem to be stuck in a Sartrean bar in which a tedious stranger subjects us to an endless harangue concerning his personal failures. Russell Jacoby reports the conclusions of a 1985 *Chronicle of Higher Education* article that estimated that 40 percent of the nation's faculty are ready to leave the academy. The reason: boredom (*The Last Intellectuals: American Culture in the Age of Academe*, p. xiii).

We have come through a period that has offered a set of interesting paradigms constructed by a small handful of thinkers. To academicians this is raw meat, but what they make of it is often bland and undistinguished (and undistinguishable). Each year the popular press reports on absurdist session topics at the annual MLA convention; the right wing wrings its hands at the perceived threats to all that is holy and the general public shakes its collective head in confusion and misunderstanding. The real sufferers, however, are those who attend the actual talks and look on as potentially important or interesting subjects are ground down to fragments of tedious trivia or presented in the most predictable of fashions.

I remember a directive that was once sent to our graduate students concerning the MLA job market; it included a comment to the effect that the principal purpose of the annual convention of the Modern Language Association is the "exchange of scholarly information." I would not say that scholarly information is never exchanged at such meetings, but the percentage of time, space, and energy devoted to the actual exchange of *new* information or to the presentation of a bona fide new or fresh approach is miniscule. Anyone who claims that the contrary is true is either dishonest or so radically uninformed that the presentations are new to him or her alone. Much the same is true when one turns to the vast majority of literary, scholarly journals. There are gains from time to time, but the increments are so small that the cost/benefit ratio between the energy invested and the product received has become increasingly intolerable.

This is not a new development. It is a development that is exacerbated as specialization and professionalization increase. It is a development that is exacerbated as fewer and fewer individuals with external-world experience enter the academy. It is a development that is exacerbated as a constricted academic job market drives able students to professional schools instead of doctoral programs and renders those who remain increasingly fearful. Many have pointed to Maynard Mack's suggestion a generation ago that 95 percent of every year's work was worthless and should be burned at the year's end. That percentage has now risen and it will continue to rise if the conditions that produce it are not changed.

There is a further problem attending research that is either hopelessly minor or hopelessly imitative and derivative: it will have little or no impact on the undergraduate classroom. Undergraduates are energized by basic research. The pursuit of important topics and the use of truly innovative approaches stretch the researcher and extend his or her abilities as a teacher.

The debate between the relative importance of teaching and research is an idle one only when the research is significant. The pursuit of trivial subjects or the pursuit of important subjects in trivial ways neither advances knowledge in any important way nor enriches the undergraduate classroom. There is an old saying to the effect that all academic writing eventually gets published, once it finds its proper level. It is possible to create whole departments of individuals with lengthy bibliographies whose work is largely unknown to colleagues and largely meaningless to students, for the simple reason that it appears in journals of such justifiably small circulation and/or visibility that it is existentially nonexistent. The only justification for such work, as far as I can see, is that it has forced the author, to some extent or other, to organize his or her thoughts in sufficiently coherent fashion to pass minimal editorial muster. That process of organizing ideas *may* result in their clarification and, as a result, make the person a slightly more effective teacher.

Many will, of course, cry foul at this charge, but anyone who has undertaken an extended research project has been forced to read what is, in effect, the same article (or book) over and over again. The economy of the profession encourages the writing of such material; universities publish new journals in the interest of acquiring reputations and commercial houses publish them in the interest of acquiring money. In the sciences, authors are expected to pay page-costs in addition to asking their libraries to pay high subscription rates for those journals in which they publish what is, after all, financially subsidized work. At least the humanities have not yet reached that point.

What might one suggest as a possible alternative to current practice? It is not enough to ask for work that is fresh and important, for those characteristics are always desired. I would suggest, as one of many possible alternatives, the activity that attracted Johnson. It is quite clear and quite generally recognized that Johnson's interest in literature was not, ultimately, aesthetic. He recognized art, he created art, and he praised art, but he principally went to books to learn of men and of life. As I pointed out earlier, his interest was in what we would call the psychological or—forgetting for a moment its unfavorable associations—the behavioral. His practice recalls Murray Krieger's opinion that every humanist ought to be a cultural anthropologist.

Johnson was fascinated by the things that human beings do and the reasons why they do them. Thus, he saw literature as a part—and *only* a part—of the totality of human experience. To follow him in his methods and pursuits is to abandon narrow specialization; it is, further, to err in the direction of breadth rather than in that of depth. Krutch, not understanding what Johnson was really about, described his reading as "casual" and "unsystematic." Of course, that type of reading is at the heart of Johnson's accomplishment. Johnson follows his human subject wherever that subject leads, and he marshals all of his knowledge—of chemistry, medicine, law, numismatics, military history, whatever—to understand it.

His subject is nothing less than human life itself, and while that may be too broad a subject for a dissertation or a semester-long course, Johnson's success as a literary commentator suggests that a broad education and a broad view of the humanities could yield a particularly memorable body of commentary on specific human artifacts and specific human phenomena. As we eschew desiccating specialization, we should broaden the materials at our disposal. I would refer again to Pelikan's point that breakthroughs in research come from broad, general education; they do not come from narrow specialization, since the specialists are all following the same track and need to be shown a new set of possibilities. For example, the materials that Johnson used certainly included the products of popular culture. His reading and observation were by no means confined by highbrow professionalism but ranged across the materials available in the print and material culture of his day.

He prized experience. Shakespeare, it is clear to Johnson, has seen that which he describes. He praised Fanny Burney's *Evelina* over Pope's *Windsor Forest*, arguing that *Evelina* required of its author a knowledge of life and manners, accuracy of observation, and skill of penetration (Brown, p. 300). He had no fear of the world; he immersed himself in it, commenting that if he ever left London he would live at Aberdeen rather than Oxford, "for Aberdeen is not only a seat of learning, but a seat of Commerce, which would be particularly agreeable" (Page, p. 115). Johnson, it is clear, would agree with Wallace Stevens's comment that "the imagination loses vitality as it ceases to adhere to what is real" (Stevens, p. 6), a view that recapitulates the Goethean point that it is far better to attempt to make the real poetic than to make the poetic real.

I argued earlier that Johnson combines an active whimsy with a posture of high seriousness, that he never relinquishes his sense of purpose or his often-unexpected playfulness. While we are capable of high seriousness, certainly of the appearance of it, we have greater difficulty in applying it to what might appear to be more commonplace subject matter or—the flip side—handling the more serious subject matter with a light touch.

Barthes is an exception here, of course, but to encompass Johnson is to move beyond the accomplishments of Barthes and those of at least a half-dozen other writers. The inclusiveness of his attitudes is paralleled by the inclusiveness of his behaviors. He is part Barthes, part Edmund Wilson, part Isaac Asimov, part Sir James Murray, part Winters and Eliot and Frye, part Leslie Fiedler, and perhaps part Habermas and even Raymond Williams.

We might linger for a moment on the experience of Fiedler—a signature figure for Brian McCrea. Fiedler labored for years on the academic margins and was often treated with some contempt by the academic establishment, in part, no doubt, because he knew so many more books than did his critics. He wrote for a broad audience from the beginning, and his insights, radical and shocking to some in their time, now appear quite acceptable, perhaps even commonplace. One recent attendee of the English Institute commented that Fiedler was the least radical individual there—radical referring, of course, to his literary posture. In terms of following his own lights at great professional cost, of course, Fiedler makes most of the current "radicals" look like gray-flannel professionals.

Fiedler is one of the few literary academics ever to appear on mass-audience television and seem comfortable there. Moreover, his appearances have often been concerned with actual work, his book on freaks, for example, while many appearances by literary academics now are really issue-oriented or pseudo-issue oriented, as in the discussions of gossipy topics like political correctness, which bear the kind of relationship to scholarship in the humanities that the gays-in-the-military issue bears to national defense or military history.

It has been interesting to watch Fiedler range across literary history and cultural history at the same time that he has often anchored himself in the study of particular figures; one thinks, for example, of his ongoing interest in Twain. His heavily classical education has served as a solid backdrop for cultural studies, which at first glance appear to be remote from his personal training, and he is one of the relatively few academics who has written a serious body of fiction. He might be one of the last individuals who would leap to mind if one were thinking of modern inheritors of the Johnsonian way, but the more one considers the facts of his career, the more one might be persuaded that he is one of the most Johnsonian of modern literary writers.

One of the most obvious characteristics of contemporary literary study is the desire to broaden the list of materials under investigation. Such a desire is not only encompassed but encouraged by Johnson's approach—providing we do not lose sight of our purposes: to explore the human condition, human behaviors, and the manner in which those have been represented and, hence, understood. Literature is subordinate to life, a point on which those at opposite ends of the political spectrum might be persuaded to agree.

Certainly one sees the results of a Johnsonian perspective all around us. Literary history increasingly explores the experiences (and representations of those experiences) of a multiplicity of the members of the human family. Social history now dominates historiography in ways that could not have been foreseen as late as a generation ago, and biography is being practiced with great expertness. Genre writing has a large audience and a serious array of skilled practitioners.

Any of these activities can be overdone and important issues forgotten in the process, but the Johnsonian perspective is far more in evidence today than it might at first glance appear to be. If we have lost a part of the classical side of Johnson we have at least gained the forward-looking, populist side of him. There is, I believe, a strong reason for this, one that I have held in abeyance until now.

Quo Vadis?

The death of literature—much-discussed now and in some circles much-celebrated, in others much-lamented—is not, in any sense of the term, a recent event. Literature with a capital *L* really died with the aristocracy that consumed it. Like the death of the aristocracy itself, the process has been a lingering one, but it can be dated from the late Renaissance. With the Renaissance came the emergence of a powerful and literate middle class that produced, in place of Literature, Writing. Its principal forms were the novel and the periodical essay, the latter now dispersed and displaced but still a significant part of the literary landscape, the former the dominant literary form. (I exclude such things as religious writings, which were extremely popular both prior to and after the rise of the novel, since they transcend class in a number of ways. They remain important today, though there is some displacement into New Age materials of various kinds, from the significant to the silly.)

Poetry was killed by the universities, but since the general public would not permit the death of rhymed narrative it displaced into popular music, a set of events that occurred in very convenient tandem, with the rise of popular music paralleling the expansion of universities because of the G.I. bill and the 1957 .45 to the temple that was Sputnik. The music spread and prospered just as the universities expanded, devouring traditional poetry along the way.

The creation of the English industry—the development of English teaching in nineteenth-century Mechanics' Institutes—came two centuries after the events that presaged it. It is very interesting now to remember the rationale for the creation of English studies, namely the belief that the masses were incapable of studying Latin and Greek and should be given something in their stead with which they could reasonably deal. Since then we have seen the traditional English canon be viewed as a hegemonic instrument rather than the populist instrument it was originally intended to be, but the real bottom line was apparent from the beginning: the nonaristocratic would study different materials than their betters. Indeed they would. Indeed they have. Indeed they have been creating different materials and consuming different materials since the Renaissance.

John G. Cawelti has suggested that the rise of the detective story is, in part, a response to the breakdown of the aristocracy and the erosion of the authority of the church. The gothic novel neatly locates the cause of middle-class fears in the lubricious hearts of monks and lords who are still about and who prey upon virginal middle-class girls, just as their forebears preyed upon entire societies. Largely gone, they are far from being forgotten. The middle class counterattacks with the detective's rationalism, the supreme antidote to superstition and arbitrary authority. This is another nineteenth-century response to a seventeenth-century phenomenon, but the continued success of the form suggests its deep cultural resonance. Interestingly, the form splits into an English and American version: the English mystery (or "cozy" in the trade) and the hard-boiled American narrative. The first is a conservative form, close, as George Grella and others have argued, to what Frye termed the argument of comedy. The American version, as defined by Chandler, is, on the other hand, related to romance.

Two observations: first, the cozy as a form is owned by women, from Agatha Christie to Margery Allingham, Ngaio Marsh, Dorothy Sayers, Mary Roberts Rinehart, down to Martha Grimes, Ruth Rendell, and P. D. James in our own time. Nevertheless, the form has received scant scholarly attention, including attention from feminists. Those who believe with Thomas Sowell that the academy is not serious about heeding the voices of black and women writers when those voices are conservative can point to the relative silence with regard to this vast (and vastly influential) body of writing. Second, while the hard-boiled narrative has been the property of male writers (with some notable exceptions, including the softer-boiled Sue Grafton and Sara Paretsky [working from the Ross Macdonald tradition more than the Chandler]), the form has been decidedly countercultural, finding evil wherever the detective turns, particularly in the institutions of government and society (which, in the cozy, are the props against evil rather than its embodiment). Chandler's knight is consciously detached from the aristocracy even though his commoner/protagonist's name was a conscious echo of Sir Thomas Malory's. If these knights are not to be found in palaces, neither are they to be found in churches, a rare exception being Lawrence Block's tithing Matt Scudder, who admits to having forgotten how he ever started the practice and who is not strictly denominational when he does it. This may be an echo of the notion of the church as legal sanctuary, providing a haven for the innocent from a corrupt government and a corrupt system of law enforcement.

While the forms that anticipate these genres are pre-novelistic, their

Quo Vadis?

success represents a novelistic response to two dying, pre-novelistic embodiments of authority, a response whose flowering comes centuries after the fact. I believe that it is safe to assume that Johnson would feel very much at home with these forms, though the only anticipations that would have been common during his time were criminal biographies, the often pornographic *Newgate Calendar*, and such things as journalistic accounts of investigations of alleged witchcraft. He himself investigated the Cock Lane "ghost" and, with Defoe and Boswell, had an interest in supernatural phenomena. He was, of course, the plausible protagonist for the mystery stories of Lillian de la Torre (Mrs. George McCue), who died recently.

In short, Johnson's immersion in a world of Writing rather than a world of Literature, a world of writers rather than "authors," constitutes the first, significant critical response to a changed situation by an individual who was both learned and populist, both classically educated and poor, open to both high culture and low, and, by the way, supportive of women and, as we now say, "minorities," both in theory and in deed. Dryden is here Janus-faced, fond of native English writing but selecting the dull and (neo)classically structured *Epicoene* as a model play. The other major writers of the age, Pope and Swift, are reactionary in this regard, their reaction sufficiently strong, in fact, to be defining elements of their thought and work. Interestingly, the period's other truly great figure, Hume, manages to be both personally conservative, intellectually forward-looking, and morally middle-class, while Boswell—another bellwether character—rather than being Johnson's alter ego, as he is sometimes represented, or his intellectual (surrogate) son, is in fact Johnson's polar opposite. Boswell is the character whose existence in nature many have denied. He is a bona fide "pre-romantic," a solipsist who is also a reactionary with a sweet tooth for sentimentalized feudalism, an individual who both imagined castles in the air and then (as he himself confessed) attempted to live in them.

Among many other things, romanticism is, after all, an attempted interruption of this process of moving from Literature to Writing, a substitution of intellectual elitism for social elitism. It is for the few, not for the many, and its focus falls upon the unique and ineffable, not the common and mutually shared. It always looks backward rather than forward, back to childhood, back to Eden, back to England's green and pleasant land. What is lost is, often, faith. Hence the locus of the search is frequently a church, a phenomenon Christopher Clausen refers to as "Tinternambulism" (p. 49).

At the time of romanticism's greatest triumphs, however, the novel not only persisted but flowered, and it successfully sustained the ethos of the Writer until our own time when romanticism displaced into academic life-in-consciousness and offered up its most predictable end product: apolitical theorizing by a would-be intellectual aristocracy embodying its thought in language purposely designed to exclude common readers. This aristocracy often bears the same relationship to the external world's interests in art and writing that the decayed monarchies bear to the contemporary world's political realities, but the intellectual aristocrats have been far more fortunate than their monarchical counterparts, since the general public—growing increasingly more skeptical and restive, it should be noted—has ceded to them a healthy share of the means of production. It has given them credentialing authority over its daughters and sons. This power—combined with the size that naturally accompanies such authority in a society such as our own—has helped to perpetuate the flavor and some of the norms of the romantic ethos long beyond the time of its earlier-predicted demise. The success of this effort has, in fact, been impressive, even as it has turned into decadence.

We continue, to a considerable extent, to live within the decadence, but that decadence is proving to be increasingly short-lived, as popular culture, particularly imagistic and electronic popular culture, completes its seductions. The fear of some is that the academy will persist in its folly and not become wise, or, at least, engaged. History would argue otherwise. What the academy is far more likely to do is simply change ruts and follow new messiahs, imitating *them* assiduously. For the moment it might be gadflies like Fish, looking at relationships between literature and law, or open-minded Marxists like Jameson, defining postmodernism with cinematic and architectural examples, or the neo-Fiedlerian Tompkins perhaps, or even a Baudrillard or Lyotard.

Johnson's example is a daunting alternative, but it is nevertheless a clear alternative: an empiricism rooted in both broad, classical learning and equally broad popular experience; a systematic but largely atheoretical focus upon a vast array of writing and a very small number of critical commentaries; a method that is largely comparative, whose goal is to both achieve pleasure and understanding—to better enable the reader to both enjoy and endure life; an approach that is inclusive rather than exclusive, populist rather than elitist, psychological and humane rather than narrowly aesthetic. If we cannot, realistically, model our actual behavior upon his, we can at least follow the directions of his thought and writing and attend to the most important lesson that he would offer us. Like Bloom—another difficult example for the average individual to follow—Johnson would encourage us to do all that we can to, finally, be ourselves, an endeavor that, under the present dispensation, will require as much courage as learning. If more were to attempt to do that, literary study would be enlivened as well as enriched.

BIBLIOGRAPHY
INDEX

BIBLIOGRAPHY

Abrams, M. H. "The Limits of Pluralism—II: The Deconstructive Angel." *Critical Inquiry* 3 (1977): 425–38.
———. *The Mirror and the Lamp: Romantic Theory and the Critical Tradition*. New York: Oxford University Press, 1953.
———. *Natural Supernaturalism: Tradition and Revolution in Romantic Literature*. New York: Norton, 1971.
Adams, Hazard, ed. *Critical Theory since Plato*. New York: Harcourt, Brace, Jovanovich, 1971.
———. "How Departments Commit Suicide." In *Profession 83*. New York: Modern Language Association, 1983.
———. *The Interests of Criticism: An Introduction to Literary Theory*. New York: Harcourt, Brace and World, 1969.
Adelman, Clifford. *Tourists in Our Own Land: Cultural Literacies and the College Curriculum*. United States Office of Education, 1992.
Allen, Don Cameron. *The Ph.D. in English and American Literature*. New York: Holt, Rinehart and Winston, 1968.
Allen, Henry. "Camille Paglia's Mad, Mad Worldview." *Washington Post*, April 15, 1991, B1, B4.
Applebome, Peter. "Comparative Literature: Times May Change, but the Writers Students Read Stay Much the Same." *New York Times*, March 1, 1995, B8.
Atlas, James. "The Battle of the Books." *New York Times Magazine*, June 5, 1988, 24–27, 72–73, 75, 85, 94.
Ayer, A. J. *The Meaning of Life*. New York: Scribner's, 1990.
———. *Wittgenstein*. London: Weidenfeld and Nicolson, 1985.
Bakhtin, M. M. *The Dialogic Imagination: Four Essays*. Ed. Michael Holquist. Trans. Caryl Emerson and Michael Holquist. Austin: University of Texas Press, 1981.
Baldick, Chris. "Talking Among Themselves." *Times Literary Supplement*, November 6–12, 1987, 1217–18.
Barnouw, Erik. *Tube of Plenty: The Evolution of American Television*. 2d rev. ed. New York: Oxford University Press, 1990.
Barrell, John. *The Dark Side of the Landscape: The Rural Poor in English Painting, 1730–1840*. Cambridge: Cambridge University Press, 1980.
Barthes, Roland. "The Death of the Author." In *Falling into Theory: Conflicting Views on Reading Literature*, ed. David H. Richter. Boston: Bedford Books, 1994.

Bibliography

Bartley, William Warren, III. *Wittgenstein.* 2d ed. Lasalle, Ill.: Open Court, 1985.
Barzun, Jacques. *The Culture We Deserve.* Ed. Arthur Krystal. Middletown, Conn.: Wesleyan University Press, 1989.
Bate, Walter Jackson. *The Achievement of Samuel Johnson.* New York: Oxford University Press, 1955.
——. "The Crisis in English Studies." *Harvard Magazine,* September-October 1982, 46–53.
Benjamin, Walter. "The Work of Art in the Age of Mechanical Reproduction." 1936. Rpt. in *Illuminations,* trans. Harry Zohn. New York: Schocken, 1969.
Bennett, William J. *To Reclaim a Legacy: A Report on the Humanities in Higher Education.* Washington: National Endowment for the Humanities, 1984.
Bettelheim, Bruno. *The Uses of Enchantment: The Meaning and Importance of Fairy Tales.* New York: Knopf, 1977.
Bloom, Allan. *The Closing of the American Mind: How Higher Education Has Failed Democracy and Impoverished the Souls of Today's Students.* New York: Simon and Schuster, 1987.
Bloom, Harold. *The Anxiety of Influence: A Theory of Poetry.* New York: Oxford University Press, 1973.
Boorstin, Daniel J. *The Discoverers.* New York: Random House, 1983.
——. *The Image: A Guide to Pseudo-Events in America.* New York: Atheneum, 1987.
Boswell, James. *Boswell's Journal of A Tour to the Hebrides with Samuel Johnson, L.L.D.* Ed. Frederick A. Pottle and Charles H. Bennett. New York: Literary Guild, 1936.
——. *Boswell's Life of Johnson.* Ed. G. B. Hill. Rev. and enl. by L. F. Powell. 6 vols. Oxford: Clarendon, 1934, 1950.
Bowie, Malcolm. *Lacan.* London: Fontana, 1991.
Boyd, John D. *The Function of Mimesis and Its Decline.* New York: Fordham University Press, 1980.
Brown, Joseph Epes. *Critical Opinions of Samuel Johnson.* Princeton: Princeton University Press, 1926.
Burke, Kenneth. "Literature as Equipment for Living." In *Critical Theory since Plato,* ed. Hazard Adams. New York: Harcourt, Brace, Jovanovich, 1971.
Burke, Seán. *The Death and Return of the Author: Criticism and Subjectivity in Barthes, Foucault, and Derrida.* Edinburgh: Edinburgh University Press, 1992.
Cage, Mary Crystal. "Survey Finds That Most English Departments Include Classical Texts in Lower-Division Courses." *Chronicle of Higher Education* 40 (1994): A18.

Bibliography

Campbell, Colin. "The Tyranny of the Yale Critics." *New York Times Magazine*, February 9, 1986, 20-28, 43, 47-48.

Carpenter, Lucas. "Academic Poetry That Has No Place in the Real World." *Chronicle of Higher Education* 40 (1994): A44.

Cawelti, John G. *Adventure, Mystery, and Romance: Formula Stories as Art and Popular Culture.* Chicago: University of Chicago Press, 1976.

Cheney, Lynne V. *Humanities in America: Report to the President, the Congress, and the American People.* Washington, D.C.: National Endowment for the Humanities, 1988.

Cixous, Hèléne. "The Laugh of the Medusa." Trans. Keith Cohen and Paula Cohen. *Signs* 1 (1976): 875-94.

Clausen, Christopher. *The Place of Poetry: Two Centuries of an Art in Crisis.* Lexington: University Press of Kentucky, 1981.

Cochrane, J. A. *Dr. Johnson's Printer: The Life of William Strahan.* Cambridge: Harvard University Press, 1964.

Collins, A. S. *Authorship in the Days of Johnson: Being a Study of the Relation Between Author, Patron, Publisher and Public, 1726-1780.* London: Routledge, 1927.

Corrigan, Timothy. *A Cinema Without Walls: Movies and Culture after Vietnam.* New Brunswick, N.J.: Rutgers University Press, 1991.

Crane, R. S. "Criticism as Inquiry; or, The Perils of the 'High Priori Road.'" In *The Idea of the Humanities and Other Essays Critical and Historical.* Chicago: University of Chicago Press, 1967.

——. "English Neoclassical Criticism: An Outline Sketch." In *Dictionary of World Literature*, ed. Joseph T. Shipley. New York: Philosophical Library, 1943.

——. *The Language of Criticism and the Structure of Poetry.* Toronto: University of Toronto Press, 1953.

Crawford, Donald W. *Kant's Aesthetic Theory.* Madison: University of Wisconsin Press, 1974.

Crews, Frederick. "In the Big House of Theory." *New York Review of Books*, May 29, 1986, 36-42.

Crumley, James. *The Mexican Tree Duck.* New York: Mysterious Press, 1993.

Culler, Jonathan. *On Deconstruction: Theory and Criticism after Structuralism.* Ithaca: Cornell University Press, 1982.

——. *The Pursuit of Signs: Semiotics, Literature, Deconstruction.* Ithaca: Cornell University Press, 1981.

——. *Structuralist Poetics: Structuralism, Linguistics, and the Study of Literature.* Ithaca: Cornell University Press, 1976.

Damrosch, Leopold, Jr. *The Uses of Johnson's Criticism.* Charlottesville: University Press of Virginia, 1976.

Danto, Arthur C. *The Transfiguration of the Commonplace: A Philosophy of Art*. Cambridge: Harvard University Press, 1981.

Davie, Donald. "Criticism and the Academy." In *Criticism in the University*, ed. Gerald Graff and Reginald Gibbons. Evanston: Northwestern University Press, 1985.

De Man, Paul. *Allegories of Reading*. New Haven: Yale University Press, 1979.

———. *Blindness and Insight*. New York: Oxford University Press, 1971.

———. *Paul de Man: Wartime Journalism, 1939–1943*. Ed. Werner Hamacher, Neil Hertz, and Thomas Keenan. Lincoln: University of Nebraska Press, 1988.

Derrida, Jacques. *Dissemination*. Trans. Barbara Johnson. Chicago: University of Chicago Press, 1981.

———. *Of Grammatology*. Trans. Gayatri Spivak. Baltimore: Johns Hopkins University Press, 1974.

Donner, H. W. "Dr. Johnson as a Literary Critic." *Edda* 54 (1954): 325–37.

Donoghue, Denis. "Deconstructing Deconstruction." *New York Review of Books*, June 12, 1980, 37–41.

Drabelle, Dennis. "A Look at Popularization as an Academic Pursuit." *Scholarly Communication* 6 (1986): 6–9.

D'Souza, Dinesh, "Illiberal Education." *Atlantic Monthly* 267 (1991): 51–58, 62–65, 67, 70–74, 76, 78–79.

———. *Illiberal Education: The Politics of Race and Sex on Campus*. New York: Free Press, 1991.

Eagleton, Terry. *The Function of Criticism: From* The Spectator *to Post-Structuralism*. London: Verso, 1984.

———. *The Illusions of Postmodernism*. Oxford: Blackwell, 1996.

———. *Literary Theory: An Introduction*. Minneapolis: University of Minnesota Press, 1983.

———. *Walter Benjamin, or Towards a Revolutionary Criticism*. London: New Left Books, 1981.

Eliot, T. S. "Johnson as Critic and Poet." In *On Poetry and Poets*. New York: Noonday, 1957.

Ellis, John M. *Against Deconstruction*. Princeton: Princeton University Press, 1989.

———. "The Origins of PC." *Chronicle of Higher Education* 38 (1992): B1–B2.

———. *The Theory of Literary Criticism: A Logical Analysis*. Berkeley and Los Angeles: University of California Press, 1974.

Engell, James, ed. *Johnson and His Age*. Cambridge: Harvard University Press, 1984.

Fiedler, Leslie. *Love and Death in the American Novel*. New York: Stein and Day, 1960.

―――. *What Was Literature? Class Culture and Mass Society*. New York: Simon and Schuster, 1982.
Field, Syd. *Screenplay: The Foundations of Screenwriting*. New York: Delta, 1979.
Finkel, David. "Group Portrait with Television." *Washington Post Magazine*, January 16, 1994, 10–15, 24–27.
Fischer, Michael. *Does Deconstruction Make Any Difference? Poststructuralism and the Defense of Poetry in Modern Criticism*. Bloomington: Indiana University Press, 1985.
Fish, Stanley. *Is There a Text in This Class? The Authority of Interpretive Communities*. Cambridge: Harvard University Press, 1980.
―――. *Self-Consuming Artifacts: The Experience of Seventeenth-Century Literature*. Berkeley and Los Angeles: University of California Press, 1972.
―――. *Surprised by Sin: The Reader in* Paradise Lost. 2d ed. Berkeley and Los Angeles: University of California Press, 1971.
Fleeman, J. D. "The Revenue of a Writer: Samuel Johnson's Literary Earnings." In *Studies in the Book Trade in Honour of Graham Pollard*. Oxford: Oxford Bibliographical Society, 1975.
Foucault, Michel. *Discipline and Punish*. Trans. Alan Sheridan. New York: Pantheon, 1978.
―――. *The History of Sexuality*. Vol. 1. Trans. Robert Hurley. New York: Pantheon, 1978.
―――. *Madness and Civilization: A History of Insanity in the Age of Reason*. Trans. Richard Howard. New York: Random House, 1965.
Friedrich, Otto. *City of Nets: A Portrait of Hollywood in the 1940's*. New York: Harper and Row, 1986.
Frye, Northrop. *Anatomy of Criticism: Four Essays*. Princeton: Princeton University Press, 1957.
―――. "Literary and Linguistic Scholarship in a Postliterate World." *PMLA* 99 (1984): 990–95.
―――. *A Study of English Romanticism*. New York: Random House, 1968.
Fukuyama, Francis. *The End of History and the Last Man*. New York: Free Press, 1992.
Fussell, Paul. *The Rhetorical World of Augustan Humanism: Ethics and Imagery from Swift to Burke*. London: Oxford University Press, 1965.
Gardner, Helen. *In Defence of the Imagination*. Cambridge: Harvard University Press, 1982.
Geertz, Clifford. *The Interpretation of Cultures*. New York: Basic Books, 1973.
Gerhart, Mary. *The Question of Belief in Literary Criticism: An Introduction to the Hermeneutical Theory of Paul Ricoeur*. Stuttgart: Akademischer Verlag Hans-Dieter Heinz, 1979.

Gilbert, Sandra, and Susan Gubar. *The Madwoman in the Attic: The Woman Writer and the Nineteenth-Century Literary Imagination.* New Haven: Yale University Press, 1979.
Gitlin, Todd. *Inside Prime Time.* New York: Pantheon, 1983.
———. *The Twilight of Common Dreams: Why America Is Wracked by Culture Wars.* New York: Metropolitan Books, 1995.
Gleick, James. *Genius: The Life and Science of Richard Feynman.* New York: Pantheon, 1992.
Goodheart, Eugene. *The Failure of Criticism.* Cambridge: Harvard University Press, 1978.
———. *The Skeptic Disposition in Contemporary Criticism.* Princeton: Princeton University Press, 1984.
Graff, Gerald. *Beyond the Culture Wars.* New York: Norton, 1992.
———. *Literature Against Itself: Literary Ideas in Modern Society.* Chicago: University of Chicago Press, 1979.
———. *Professing Literature: An Institutional History.* Chicago: University of Chicago Press, 1987.
Graff, Gerald, and Reginald Gibbons, eds. *Criticism in the University.* Evanston: Northwestern University Press, 1985.
Greene, Donald. *Samuel Johnson.* Updated ed. Boston: Twayne Publishers, 1989.
———, ed. *Samuel Johnson.* Oxford: Oxford University Press, 1984.
———. "Samuel Johnson and the Great War for Empire." In *English Writers of the Eighteenth Century*, ed. John H. Middendorf. New York: Columbia University Press, 1971.
Greer, Germaine. *The Female Eunuch.* New York: McGraw-Hill, 1971.
Groden, Michael, and Martin Kreiswirth, eds. *The Johns Hopkins Guide to Literary Theory and Criticism.* Baltimore: Johns Hopkins University Press, 1994.
Gross, Gloria Sybil. "Johnson and the Uses of Enchantment." In *Fresh Reflections on Samuel Johnson: Essays in Criticism*, ed. Prem Nath. Troy, N.Y.: Whitston, 1987.
Habermas, Jürgen. *The Structural Transformation of the Public Sphere: An Inquiry into a Category of Bourgeois Society.* Trans. Thomas Burger with the assistance of Frederick Lawrence. Cambridge: MIT Press, 1989.
Hagstrum, Jean H. "Samuel Johnson among the Deconstructionists." *Georgia Review* 39 (1985): 537–47.
———. *Samuel Johnson's Literary Criticism.* Minneapolis: University of Minnesota Press, 1952.
Haining, Peter, ed. *The Fantastic Pulps.* New York: Vintage, 1976.
Hamacher, Werner, Neil Hertz, and Thomas Keenan. *Responses on Paul de Man's Wartime Journalism.* Lincoln: University of Nebraska Press, 1989.

Bibliography

Hardison, O. B., Jr. "The De-meaning of Meaning." *Sewanee Review* 91 (1983): 397–405.

———. *Disappearing Through the Skylight: Culture and Technology in the Twentieth Century*. New York: Viking, 1989.

Harkness, Bruce. "Bibliography and the Novelistic Fallacy." *Studies in Bibliography* 12 (1959): 59–73.

Harris, Thomas. *The Silence of the Lambs*. New York: St. Martin's, 1988.

Hartman, Geoffrey. *Criticism in the Wilderness*. New Haven: Yale University Press, 1980.

Hill, George Birkbeck. "Dr. Johnson as a Radical." *Contemporary Review* 55 (1889): 888–99.

Hinnant, Charles H. *"Steel for the Mind": Samuel Johnson and Critical Discourse*. Newark: University of Delaware Press, 1994.

Hirsch, David H. "The New Theoreticism." *Sewanee Review* 91 (1983): 417–25.

———. "Paul de Man and the Politics of Deconstruction." *Sewanee Review* 96 (1988): 330–38.

Hirsch, E. D., Jr. "Cultural Literacy." *American Scholar* 52 (1983): 159–69.

———. *Cultural Literacy: What Every American Needs to Know*. Boston: Houghton-Mifflin, 1987.

———. *Validity in Interpretation*. New Haven: Yale University Press, 1967.

Hodges, Andrew. *Alan Turing: The Enigma*. New York: Simon and Schuster, 1983.

Hongo, Garrett and Catherine N. Parke. "A Conversation with Sandra M. Gilbert." *Missouri Review* 9 (1986): 89–109.

Hume, David. *An Inquiry Concerning Human Understanding*. Ed. Charles W. Hendel. New York: Liberal Arts Press, 1955.

Hunter, J. Paul. *Before Novels: The Cultural Contexts of Eighteenth-Century English Fiction*. New York: Norton, 1990.

———. "The Novel and the Contexts of Discourse." In *Theory and Tradition in Eighteenth-Century Studies*, ed. Richard B. Schwartz. Carbondale: Southern Illinois University Press, 1990.

Involvement in Learning. Washington, D.C.: National Institute for Education, 1984.

Jacoby, Russell. *Dogmatic Wisdom: How the Culture Wars Divert Education and Distract America*. New York: Doubleday, 1994.

———. *The Last Intellectuals: American Culture in the Age of Academe*. New York: Basic Books, 1987.

Jameson, Frederic. *Postmodernism, or, the Cultural Logic of Late Capitalism*. Durham: Duke University Press, 1991.

Johnson, Charles. *Middle Passage*. New York: Atheneum, 1990.

Johnson, Paul. *Intellectuals*. New York: Harper and Row, 1988.

Johnson, Samuel. *The Letters of Samuel Johnson*. Ed. Bruce Redford. 5 vols. Princeton: Princeton University Press, 1992–94.

———. *Lives of the English Poets.* Ed. G. B. Hill. 3 vols. Oxford: Clarendon Press, 1905.

———. *The Works of Samuel Johnson, LL.D. Together with his Life, and Notes on his Lives of the Poets. By Sir John Hawkins, Knt.* 11 vols. London: J. Buckland, J. Rivington, et al., 1787.

———. *The Yale Edition of the Works of Samuel Johnson.* General ed., Allen T. Hazen; from 1966, John H. Middendorf. New Haven: Yale University Press, 1958–.

Jones, Lyle V., et al., eds. *An Assessment of Research-Doctorate Programs in the United States: Humanities.* Washington, D.C.: National Academy Press, 1982.

Kahler, Erich. *The Inward Turn of Narrative.* Trans. Richard and Clara Winston. Princeton: Princeton University Press, 1973.

Kant, Immanuel. *Critique of Pure Reason.* Trans. F. Max Müller. New York: Anchor, 1966.

Kazin, Alfred. *On Native Grounds: An Interpretation of Modern American Prose Literature.* New York: Harcourt, Brace, Jovanovich, 1970.

Keast, William R. "Johnson's Criticism of the Metaphysical Poets." *ELH* 17 (1950): 59–70.

———. "The Theoretical Foundations of Johnson's Criticism." In *Critics and Criticism, Ancient and Modern,* ed. R. S. Crane. Chicago: University of Chicago Press, 1952.

Kermode, Frank. "The Decline of the Man of Letters." *Partisan Review* 52 (1985): 195–209.

Kernan, Alvin. *The Death of Literature.* New Haven: Yale University Press, 1990.

Kimball, Roger. *Tenured Radicals: How Politics Has Corrupted Our Higher Education.* New York: Harper and Row, 1990.

Kinder, Marsha. *Playing with Power in Movies, Television, and Video Games.* Berkeley and Los Angeles: University of California Press, 1991.

Koenig, Rhoda. "At Play in the Fields of the Word: Alienation, Imagination, Feminism, and Foolishness at PEN." *New York,* February 3, 1986, 40–47.

Krieger, Murray. "Criticism as Secondary Art." In *What Is Criticism,* ed. Paul Hernadi. Bloomington: Indiana University Press, 1981.

———. *The Institution of Theory.* Baltimore: Johns Hopkins University Press, 1994.

———. *Words about Words about Words: Theory, Criticism, and the Literary Text.* Baltimore: Johns Hopkins University Press, 1988.

Krutch, Joseph Wood. *Samuel Johnson.* New York: Henry Holt and Co., 1944.

Kuhn, Thomas. *The Structure of Scientific Revolutions.* 2d ed. Chicago: University of Chicago Press, 1970.

Bibliography

Lacan, Jacques. *Écrits: A Selection*. Trans. Alan Sheridan. New York: Norton, 1977.

Leavis, F. R. *The Great Tradition*. Garden City: Doubleday, 1954.

———. "Johnson as Critic." *Scrutiny* 12 (1944): 187–204. Rpt. in *Samuel Johnson: A Collection of Critical Essays*, ed. Donald J. Greene. Englewood Cliffs: Prentice Hall, 1965.

Lehman, David. *Signs of the Times: Deconstruction and the Fall of Paul de Man*. New York: Poseidon, 1991.

Leibowitz, Herbert. "Amazing Gracelessness: How Jargon Has Ruined the Language of Criticism." *Thesis* 7 (1993): 4–11.

Lentricchia, Frank. *After the New Criticism*. Chicago: University of Chicago Press, 1980.

———. *Criticism and Social Change*. Chicago: University of Chicago Press, 1983.

Levine, Lawrence W. *Highbrow/Lowbrow: The Emergence of Cultural Hierarchy in America*. Cambridge: Harvard University Press, 1988.

Lewis, C. S. "De Descriptione Temporum." Inaugural lecture of the Chair of Medieval and Renaissance English Literature at Cambridge, frequently reprinted, n.d.

Lindenberger, Herbert. "Toward a New History in Literary Study." In *Profession 84*. New York: Modern Language Association, 1984.

Litz, A. Walton. "Literary Criticism." In *Harvard Guide to Contemporary American Writing*, ed. Daniel Hoffman. Cambridge: Harvard University Press, 1979.

Lodge, David. *Changing Places*. Harmondsworth: Penguin, 1979.

———. *Nice Work*. London: Secker and Warburg, 1988.

———. *Small World*. New York: Macmillan, 1984.

Lucas, F. L. *Literature and Psychology*. London: Cassell and Company, 1951.

Lynn, Steven. *Samuel Johnson after Deconstruction: Rhetoric and* The Rambler. Carbondale: Southern Illinois University Press, 1992.

Macdonald, Dwight. *Masscult and Midcult*. New York: Partisan Review, 1961.

MacDonald, J. Fred. *One Nation under Television: The Rise and Decline of Network TV*. New York: Pantheon, 1990.

Mack, John E. *A Prince of Our Disorder: The Life of T. E. Lawrence*. Boston: Little, Brown, 1976.

Matthews, Anne. "Deciphering Victorian Underwear and Other Seminars." *New York Times Magazine*, February 10, 1991, 42–43, 57–59, 69.

McConnell, Frank D. "Will Deconstruction Be the Death of Literature?" *Wilson Quarterly* 14 (1990): 99–109.

McCrea, Brian. *Addison and Steele Are Dead: The English Department, Its Canon, and the Professionalization of Literary Criticism*. Newark: University of Delaware Press, 1990.

———. "The Inevitability of Derrida." *The Scriblerian and the Kit-Cats* 18 (1985): 7–9.
McGann, Jerome J., ed. *Historical Studies and Literary Criticism*. Madison: University of Wisconsin Press, 1985.
Megill, Allan. *Prophets of Extremity: Nietzsche, Heidegger, Foucault, Derrida*. Berkeley and Los Angeles: University of California Press, 1985.
Meredith, Scott. *Writing to Sell*. 2d ed. rev. New York: Harper and Row, 1974.
Messinger, Gary S. "The Liberal Arts in Britain: Some Lessons for America." *Academe* 69 (1983): 21–27.
Miller, J. Hillis. "Tradition and Difference." Review of *Natural Supernaturalism*, by M. H. Abrams. *Diacritics* 2 (1972): 6–13.
Mish, Charles C., ed. *The Anchor Anthology of Short Fiction of the Seventeenth Century*. Garden City: Doubleday, 1963.
Mitchell, W. J. T., ed. *Against Theory: Literary Study and the New Pragmatism*. Chicago: University of Chicago Press, 1985.
Montaigne, Michel de. *The Complete Essays*. Trans. Donald M. Frame. Stanford: Stanford University Press, 1965.
Murfin, Ross C., ed. *Joseph Conrad: Heart of Darkness—A Case Study in Contemporary Criticism*. New York: St. Martin's, 1989.
Natoli, Joseph, ed. *Tracing Literary Theory*. Urbana: University of Illinois Press, 1989.
Nelson, Cary. "On Whether Criticism Is Literature." In *What Is Criticism*, ed. Paul Hernadi. Bloomington: Indiana University Press, 1981.
Nolan, William F. *The Black Mask Boys: Masters in the Hard-Boiled School of Detective Fiction*. New York: Mysterious Press, 1985.
Norris, Christopher. *Deconstruction: Theory and Practice*. London: Methuen, 1982.
———. *Derrida*. London: Fontana, 1987.
———. *What's Wrong with Postmodernism: Critical Theory and the Ends of Philosophy*. Baltimore: Johns Hopkins University Press, 1990.
Ohmann, Richard. *English in America: A Radical View of the Profession*. New York: Oxford University Press, 1976.
Page, Norman, ed. *Dr. Johnson: Interviews and Recollections*. London: Macmillan, 1987.
Paglia, Camille. "Academe Has to Recover Its Spiritual Roots and Overthrow the Ossified Political Establishment of Invested Self-Interest." *Chronicle of Higher Education* 37 (1991): B1–B2.
———. "Ninnies, Pedants, Tyrants and Other Academics." *New York Times Book Review*, May 5, 1991, 1, 29, 33.
———. *Sex, Art, and American Culture: Essays*. New York: Vintage, 1992.

Bibliography

———. *Sexual Personae: Art and Decadence from Nefertiti to Emily Dickinson*. New Haven: Yale University Press, 1990.
———. *Vamps and Tramps: New Essays*. New York: Vintage, 1994.
Palmer, D. J. *The Rise of English Studies: An Account of the Study of English Language and Literature from Its Origins to the Making of the Oxford English School*. London: Oxford University Press, 1965.
Parfrey, Adam, ed. *Apocalypse Culture*. Portland, Oreg.: Feral House, 1990.
Parker, Hershel. *Flawed Texts and Verbal Icons: Literary Authority in American Fiction*. Evanston: Northwestern University Press, 1984.
Parrinder, Patrick. *The Failure of Theory: Essays on Criticism and Contemporary Fiction*. Brighton: Harvester, 1987.
Patey, Douglas Lane. *Probability and Literary Form: Philosophic Theory and Literary Practice in the Augustan Age*. Cambridge: Cambridge University Press, 1984.
Pechter, Edward. "The New Historicism and its Discontents: Politicizing Renaissance Drama." *PMLA* 102 (1987): 292–303.
Pelikan, Jaroslav. *Scholarship and Its Survival: Questions on the Idea of Graduate Education*. N.p.: The Carnegie Foundation for the Advancement of Teaching, n.d.
Peyre, Henri. *The Failures of Criticism*. Ithaca: Cornell University Press, 1967.
Piper, William Bowman. "Samuel Johnson as an Exemplary Critic." *TSLL* 20 (1978): 457–73.
Popkin, Richard. "David Hume: His Pyrrhonism and His Critique of Pyrrhonism." 1951. Rpt. in *Hume*, ed. V. C. Chappell. New York: Doubleday, 1966.
———. *The History of Scepticism from Erasmus to Descartes*. New York: Humanities Press, 1964.
Rahv, Philip. "Paleface and Redskin." In *Image and Idea: Fourteen Essays on Literary Themes*. Norfolk, Conn.: New Directions, 1949.
Reade, Aleyn Lyell. *Johnsonian Gleanings*. 11 vols. 1909–52. Rpt., New York: Octagon Books, 1967.
"Rethinking the Canon." *LAS Newsletter*. College of Liberal Arts and Sciences, University of Illinois. Summer 1992, 5, 9.
Richter, David H. *Falling into Theory: Conflicting Views on Reading Literature*. New York: Bedford Books, 1994.
Rigney, Barbara Hill. *Madness and Sexual Politics in the Feminist Novel*. Madison: University of Wisconsin Press, 1978.
Rorty, Richard. *Essays on Heidegger and Others: Philosophical Papers*. Vol. 2. Cambridge: Cambridge University Press, 1991.
———. *Philosophy and the Mirror of Nature*. Princeton: Princeton University Press, 1979.

Ross, Andrew. *No Respect: Intellectuals and Popular Culture.* New York: Routledge, 1989.
Sabot, Richard, and John Wakeman-Linn. "Grade Inflation and Course Choice." *Journal of Economic Perspectives* 5 (1991): 159–70.
Salusinszky, Imre. *Criticism in Society.* New York: Methuen, 1987.
Schwartz, Richard B. "The Humanities, the Public, and the 'Public.'" *Washington Quarterly* 5 (1982): 157–60.
———. *Samuel Johnson and the Problem of Evil.* Madison: University of Wisconsin Press, 1975.
———. "Samuel Johnson: The Professional Writer as Critic." In *Fresh Reflections on Samuel Johnson: Essays in Criticism,* ed. Prem Nath. Troy, N.Y.: Whitston, 1987.
———, ed. *Theory and Tradition in Eighteenth-Century Studies.* Carbondale: Southern Illinois University Press, 1990.
Searle, John R. "Rationality and Realism: What Is at Stake?" *Daedalus* 122 (1993): 55–83.
———. "The Word Turned Upside Down." *New York Review of Books,* October 27, 1983, 74–79.
Shapiro, Barbara J. *Probability and Certainty in Seventeenth-Century England: A Study of the Relationships Between Natural Science, Religion, History, Law, and Literature.* Princeton: Princeton University Press, 1983.
Shaw, Peter. "Devastating Developments Are Hastening the Demise of Deconstruction in Academe." *Chronicle of Higher Education* 38 (1990): B1–B2.
———. *The War Against the Intellect: Episodes in the Decline of Discourse.* Iowa City: University of Iowa Press, 1989.
Shelley, Percy B. *Selected Poems, Essays, and Letters.* Ed. Ellsworth Barnard. New York: Odyssey, 1944.
Sigworth, Oliver F. "Johnson's *Lycidas*: The End of Renaissance Criticism." *Eighteenth-Century Studies* 1 (1967): 159–68.
Silet, Charles L. P. "The Other Side of Those Mean Streets: An Interview with Walter Mosley." *Armchair Detective* 26 (1993): 8–16.
Solomon, Robert C. *Continental Philosophy since 1750: The Rise and Fall of the Self.* Oxford: Oxford University Press, 1988.
Solzhenitsyn, Aleksandr. "How the Cult of Novelty Wrecked the 20th Century." *American Arts Quarterly* 10 (1993): 18–20.
Spigel, Lynn. *Make Room for TV: Television and the Family Ideal in Postwar America.* Chicago: University of Chicago Press, 1992.
Steiner, George. *Heidegger.* 2d ed. London: Fontana, 1992.
———. *Real Presences.* Cambridge: Cambridge University Press, 1986.
Stevens, Wallace. *The Necessary Angel: Essays on Reality and the Imagination.* New York: Vintage, 1951.
Stock, R. D. *Samuel Johnson and Neoclassical Dramatic Theory: The In-*

Bibliography

tellectual Context of the Preface to Shakespeare. Lincoln: University of Nebraska Press, 1973.
———, ed. *Samuel Johnson's Literary Criticism*. Lincoln: University of Nebraska Press, 1974.
Streitfeld, David. "Fiction Prize to 'Passage's' Charles Johnson." *Washington Post*, November 28, 1990, B1–B2.
Tate, Allen. "Johnson on the Metaphysicals." *Kenyon Review* 11 (1949): 379–94.
Taylor, Charles. *Sources of the Self: The Making of the Modern Identity*. Cambridge: Harvard University Press, 1989.
Tichi, Cecelia. *Electronic Hearth: Creating an American Television Culture*. New York: Oxford University Press, 1991.
Tillyard, E. M. W. *The Elizabethan World Picture*. New York: Macmillan, 1944.
Tompkins, Jane. *West of Everything: The Inner Life of Westerns*. New York: Oxford University Press, 1992.
Toulmin, Stephen. *Cosmopolis: The Hidden Agenda of Modernity*. New York: Free Press, 1990.
Trilling, Lionel. "The Fate of Pleasure: Wordsworth to Dostoevsky." *Literary Views* 16 (1965): 93–114.
Tucker, Nicholas. *The Child and the Book: A Psychological and Literary Exploration*. Cambridge: Cambridge University Press, 1981.
Vander Meulen, David L. "Fredson Bowers and the Eighteenth Century." *Johnsonian News Letter* 52 (1992–93): 4–12.
Vendler, Helen. "Feminism and Literature." *New York Review of Books*, May 31, 1990, 19–25; and rejoinder from Sandra Gilbert, Susan Gubar, et al., "Feminism and Literature: An Exchange," August 16, 1990, 58–59.
Wain, John, ed. *Johnson as Critic*. London: Routledge and Kegan Paul, 1973.
———, ed. *Samuel Johnson: Lives of the English Poets, A Selection*. London: Dent, 1975.
Weinbrot, Howard D. *Augustus Caesar in "Augustan" England: The Decline of a Classical Norm*. Princeton: Princeton University Press, 1978.
———. "The New Eighteenth Century and the New Mythology." *Age of Johnson* 3 (1990): 353–407.
———. "The Reader, the General, and the Particular: Johnson and Imlac in Chapter Ten of *Rasselas*." *Eighteenth-Century Studies* 5 (1971): 80–96.
Weiner, Andrew D. " 'Fierce Warres and Faithful Loues': Pattern as Structure in Book I of *The Faerie Queene*." *Huntington Library Quarterly* 37 (1973): 33–57.
Wellek, René. "Destroying Literary Studies." *New Criterion* 2 (1983): 1–8.

———. "Dr. Johnson." In *A History of Modern Criticism*. Vol. 1. New Haven: Yale University Press, 1955.
Wellek, René, and Austin Warren. *Theory of Literature*. New York: Harcourt, Brace and World, 1942.
White, Hayden. "The Absurdist Moment in Contemporary Literary Theory." In *Tropics of Discourse: Essays in Cultural Criticism*. Baltimore: Johns Hopkins University Press, 1978.
Wiles, R. M. "The Contemporary Distribution of Johnson's *Rambler*." *Eighteenth-Century Studies* 2 (1968): 155–71.
Willeford, Charles. *The Burnt Orange Heresy*. Berkeley: Black Lizard Books, 1987.
———. *The Shark-Infested Custard*. Novato, Calif.: Underwood-Miller, 1993.
Wilshire, Bruce. *The Moral Collapse of the University: Professionalism, Purity, and Alienation*. Albany: State University of New York Press, 1990.
Wilson, Edmund. *Axel's Castle: A Study in the Imaginative Literature of 1870–1930*. New York: Scribner's, 1931.
———. *Classics and Commercials: A Literary Chronicle of the Forties*. New York: Farrar, Straus and Giroux, 1950.
———. "Reëxamining Dr. Johnson." 1944. Rpt. in *Samuel Johnson: A Collection of Critical Essays*, ed. Donald J. Greene. Englewood Cliffs: Prentice Hall, 1965.
Wilson, Edward O. "Biological and Human Determinants of the Survival of Species." In *Individuality and Cooperative Action*, ed. Joseph E. Earley. Washington: Georgetown University Press, 1991.
———. *On Human Nature*. Cambridge: Harvard University Press, 1978.
Winters, Yvor. *The Anatomy of Nonsense*. Norfolk, Conn.: New Directions, 1943.
Wolfe, Tom. *From Bauhaus to Our House*. New York: Farrar, Straus and Giroux, 1981.
———. *The Painted Word*. New York: Farrar, Straus and Giroux, 1975.
Wright, Louis B. *Middle-Class Culture in Elizabethan England*. Chapel Hill: University of North Carolina Press, 1935.

INDEX

Abrams, M. H., 75, 96
Adams, Ansel, 5
Adams, Hazard, 11, 93
Adams, John, 128
Addison, Joseph, 17, 44, 53, 60, 78, 107, 145
Adelman, Clifford, 25
Adorno, Theodor, 104
Agee, James, 3
Allingham, Margery, 154
Altman, Robert, 18
Anderson, Richard C., 33
Applebome, Peter, 57
Arbuthnot, John, 16, 29
Arendt, Hannah, 119
Aristotle, 1, 8, 13, 24, 46, 75
Arnold, Matthew, 10, 46, 47, 54, 78, 119
Asimov, Isaac, 23, 151
Atwood, Margaret, 108
Auden, W. H., 10, 54
Austen, Jane, 53, 108
Ayer, A. J., 42, 47, 118

Bach, Johann Sebastian, 111
Bacon, Francis, 66
Bakhtin, Mikhail, 47
Baldwin, James, 5, 54
Baraka, Amiri, 54
Barber, Francis, 145
Barnes, Barnabe, 140
Barrell, John, 98
Barth, John, 18, 91
Barthes, Roland, 19, 42, 151
Barzun, Jacques, 84, 122
Bates, Kathy, 136
Baudrillard, Jean, 133, 156
Beardsley, Monroe, 68
Beatles, the, 126
Becker, Carl, 46
Bellow, Saul, 4

Belsey, Catherine, 47
Benét, Stephen Vincent, 105
Bennett, William, 25
Bentham, Jeremy, 53
Bergen, Edgar, 103
Berkeley, George, 16, 47
Blackmore, Richard, 16, 141
Blackmur, R. P., 78
Blair, Robert, 16
Blake, William, 24–25, 53, 80
Block, Lawrence, 109, 154
Bloom, Allan, 5, 33
Bloom, Harold, 10, 46, 69, 80, 85, 87, 157
Bloomsbury Group, 54
Bonaparte, Napoleon, 96
Bond, Richmond P., 68
Boorstin, Daniel, 82, 145
Boswell, James, 16–17, 44, 54, 67, 97, 111, 155
Bowers, Fredson, 121
Brandt, Sebastian, 51
Bronson, Bertrand, 93
Brontë, Charlotte, 53
Brontë, Emily, 53
Buchwald, Art, 67
Bultmann, Rudolf, 117
Burke, Edmund, 17, 44, 53, 111
Burke, James Lee, 103, 108
Burke, Kenneth, 19, 102
Burney, Fanny, 150
Burns, Robert, 111
Butterfield, Herbert, 119
Byron, George Gordon, Lord, 44, 51, 53
Bysshe, Edward, 15

Cadzow, Hunter, 2
Cain, James M., 5
Cain, William E., 137
Campbell, Colin, 46
Campbell, Robert, 71, 109

175

Index

Capote, Truman, 72
Cassidy, Frederic, 22
Castiglione, Baldassare, 64
Castro, Fidel, 119
Cather, Willa, 3, 54
Cawelti, John G., 43, 84, 153
Cervenka, Exene, 139
Chandler, Raymond, 5, 154
Chapman, George, 42
Chatterton, Thomas, 139
Chaucer, Geoffrey, 17, 51, 53, 139
Chesterfield, Philip Dormer Stanhope, fourth earl of, 105
Christie, Agatha, 154
Churchill, Winston, 23, 128
Clausen, Christopher, 156
Clifford, James L., 121
Clinton, William J., 65
Cobban, Alfred, 119
Coburn, D. L., 137
Coleridge, Samuel Taylor, 10, 23, 51, 78, 97
Collins, Jackie, 108
Condorcet, Marie Jean Antoine Nicolas de Caritat, Marquis de, 30, 96
Conrad, Joseph, 54
Cooke, Sam, 127
Cornwallis, William, 66
Crabbe, George, 16, 98–99
Crane, Hart, 54
Crane, R. S., 2, 15, 61, 79, 85
Crawford, Donald, 93
Cromwell, Oliver, 52
Cross, Wilbur, 64
Crumley, James, 72
cummings, e. e., 54

Danielou, Jean, 119
Dante, 51
Davie, Donald, 46
Dawson, Christopher, 118
deconstruction, 69
Defoe, Daniel, 16–17, 44, 50, 53, 66, 155
de la Torre, Lillian. *See* McCue, Mrs. George
Deloney, Thomas, 99, 106

de Man, Paul, 54, 85
Dennis, John, 114
De Quincey, Thomas, 53
Derrida, Jacques, 42, 46–47, 116–18, 120, 134
Descartes, René, 11
Dickens, Charles, 42, 53, 98–99, 139
Dickinson, Emily, 4, 54
Donahue, Phil, 65
Donne, John, 53
Donoghue, Denis, 46
Dos Passos, John, 72
Dostoyevski, Fyodor, 108, 142
Drucker, Peter, 119
Dryden, 10, 46, 78, 86, 144, 155
DuBois, W. E. B., 128
Duck, Stephen, 81
Dunne, John, 118
Dunton, John, 65

Eagleton, Terry, 137, 147
Earle, John, 66
Eliot, George, 35, 44, 53, 108
Eliot, T. S., 10, 23, 28, 54, 78, 80, 144, 151
Elizabeth I, 53
Ellis, John M., 113, 133
Ellison, Harlan, 5
Ellison, Ralph, 5
Ellroy, James, 5, 72, 109
Emerson, Ralph Waldo, 4, 78
Erasmus, Desiderius, 140
Erdman, David, 53

Farrell, James T., 3–4
Faulkner, William, 3, 5–6, 54, 108
Feynman, Arline, 141
Feynman, Richard, 141
Fiedler, Leslie, 19, 22–23, 43, 64, 84, 151, 156
Field, Syd, 14
Fielding, Henry, 17, 44, 53, 86, 111, 145
Fish, Stanley, 31, 40, 47, 156
Fitzgerald, F. Scott, 3, 54, 71
Fleming, Ian, 51
Forster, E. M., 54, 69, 71
Foucault, Michel, 42, 116

Index

Frazer, James, 141
Frederick, John T., 119
Frederick II, 93
Freud, Sigmund, 141
Frye, Northrop, 24, 41, 96–97, 151, 154
Fussell, Paul, 2

Gabriel, Peter, 128
Galsworthy, John, 53
Gandhi, Mohandas K., 4
Gardner, Helen, 11
Garrick, David, 107
Gass, William, 48
Gay, John, 29, 104, 111, 137
Geertz, Clifford, 46
Gettmann, Royal, 74
Giamatti, A. Bartlett, 144
Gibbon, Edward, 17, 42, 53
Gide, André, 118
Gilbert, Sandra, 78, 82
Ginsberg, Allen, 54, 119
Gitlin, Todd, 8
Gleick, James, 141
Goethe, Johann Wolfgang von, 71, 77, 151
Goldsmith, Oliver, 16, 44, 53, 98–99, 107, 111
Goodheart, Eugene, 134
Goodman, Paul, 5
Googe, Barnabe, 140
Graff, Gerald, 36, 60, 119
Grafton, Sue, 154
Graham, Walter, 68
Gray, Thomas, 16, 86, 144
Greco, El (Domenico Teotocopulo), 51
Greenblatt, Stephen, 2
Greene, Donald J., 121
Greene, Graham, 108, 141
Grella, George, 154
Grimes, Martha, 154
Grisham, John, 29, 108
Gurian, Waldemar, 119

Habermas, Jürgen, 151
Haig, Robert L., 68
Hall, Joseph, 66
Hardison, O. B., Jr., 130–31
Hardy, Thomas, 54

Harkness, Bruce, 70
Harley, Robert, 21
Harris, Thomas, 99, 108–9, 136
Hartman, Geoffrey, 78
Harvey, Gabriel, 44
Hastings, Warren, 111
Havel, Vaclav, 18
Hawkins, Screaming Jay, 127
Hawthorne, Nathaniel, 4, 54
Haydn, Joseph, 111
Hazlitt, William, 85
Hecht, Anthony, 22
Hegel, Georg Wilhelm Friedrich, 42
Heidegger, Martin, 42, 47, 54, 116, 125
Hemingway, Ernest, 3, 105, 108
Hervey, John, Baron, 111
Hiassen, Carl, 103, 108, 110
Hill, G. B., 145
Hirsch, E. D., 31–32, 40
Hodges, Andrew, 141
Hogarth, William, 68, 104
Hollander, John, 22
Holly, Charles Hardin "Buddy," 126
Homer, 51
Hongo, Garrett, 78
Hooker, Richard, 140
Hopper, Edward, 6
Horace (Quintus Horatius Flaccus), 13, 15, 46, 75, 131, 146
Howe, Irving, 5
Hume, David, 11, 17, 30, 42, 47, 53, 94
Hunter, Evan, 103
Hunter, J. Paul, 64, 68, 135
Hurston, Zora Neale, 41

Iannone, Carol, 58
Index Librorum Prohibitorum, 117

Jacoby, Russell, 8, 26, 147
James, Henry, 6, 54, 70, 108
James, P. D., 154
Jameson, Frederic, 103, 156
Jefferson, Thomas, 128
Jenyns, Soame, 19, 116
John, Saint, the Apostle, 117
Johnson, Charles, 48
Johnson, Michael, 21
Johnson, Samuel, 1, 3–4, 6, 10–11, 13,

29–31, 42–44, 46, 50, 52–53, 67, 75, 77–78, 80, 82, 85, 93–94, 97–98, 100–101, 103, 107, 109, 111–12, 114, 125, 131, 144–45, 150
Joyce, James, 28, 54

Kames, Henry Home, Lord, 17
Kant, Immanuel, 20, 42, 74, 93, 103, 125
Kazin, Alfred, 5
Keast, William R., 18
Keats, John, 51, 75, 110
Kernan, Alvin, 1, 56, 126, 139
Kerouac, Jack, 54, 119
Keynes, John Maynard, 54
Kimball, Roger, 122, 124
Kinder, Marsha, 35, 84
King, Martin Luther, Jr., 4
King, Stephen, 29
Kirkpatrick, Sidney, 72
Kissinger, Henry, 13
Kittredge, George Lyman, 139
Kohn, Hans, 119
Kozol, Jonathan, 5
Krieger, Murray, 74, 150
Krutch, Joseph Wood, 13, 150

L'Amour, Louis, 43
Landers, Ann, 65
Larkin, Philip, 54, 108
Lavoisier, Antoine Laurent, 30, 96
Lawrence, D. H., 5, 54
Lawrence, T. E., 54, 141
Leavis, F. R., 10, 142, 144
Lentricchia, Frank, 20, 123, 137
Leonard, Elmore, 18, 51
Lewis, C. S., 24, 133
Lewis, Jerry Lee, 127
Lewis, R. W. B., 5
Lillo, George, 99, 137
Limbaugh, Rush, 47, 65
Lincoln, Abraham, 128
Llosa, Mario Vargas, 18, 100
Locke, John, 16, 42, 54
Lodge, David, 8, 91
Longinus, Dionysius, 46
Lopate, Phillip, 48

Lovejoy, A. O., 46
Lowell, Robert, 102
Lyly, John, 106
Lyotard, Jean-François, 156

Macdonald, Dwight, 5, 104, 108
Macdonald, Ross, 154
Mack, John, 141
Mack, Maynard, 148
Mackenzie, Henry, 44
Maclean, Norman, 22
MacLeish, Archibald, 105
Mallarmé, Stéphane, 47, 76, 96, 131
Malory, Thomas, 154
Mann, Thomas, 108
Marlowe, Christopher, 17
Marquez, Gabriel Garcia, 47
Marsh, Ngaio, 154
Marvell, Andrew, 17
Marxism, 35, 104, 125, 156
McBain, Ed. *See* Hunter, Evan
McConnell, Frank D., 72
McCrea, Brian, 60, 79, 151
McCue, Mrs. George, 155
McCullers, Carson, 6
McGann, Jerome, 22
McKuen, Rod, 108
McLean, Don, 126
McMillan, Terry, 48
Meeke, John, 16
Meinecke, Friedrich, 119
Melville, Herman, 4, 50, 54, 70
Meredith, Scott, 14
Miles, Josephine, 22
Mill, John Stuart, 53
Miller, Arthur, 137
Miller, Frank, 103
Miller, J. Hillis, 36
Milton, John, 40, 43, 47, 52, 80, 86, 139, 144
Mish, Charles, 106
Mitchell, Margaret, 35
Monboddo, James Burnett, Lord, 17
Montaigne, Michel Eyquem de, 38, 44, 66
Moore, Mary Tyler, 45
More, Thomas, 140

Index

Morgenthau, Hans, 119
Morris, Willie, 6
Morrison, Jim, 139
Morrison, Toni, 48, 108
Mosley, Walter, 109, 111
Mozart, Wolfgang Amadeus, 111
Murphy, Arthur, 107
Murray, Sir James, 23, 151

Nashe, Thomas, 44
Nef, John U., 119
New Criticism, 2, 69, 71, 79, 119
New Historicism, 62
Newton, Isaac, 17, 42
Nietzsche, Friedrich, 42, 47, 53, 63, 116, 120
Norris, John, 65

O'Hara, Frank, 54
O'Keeffe, Georgia, 5
Oldys, William, 21
Ornstein, Robert, 53
Orwell, George, 54, 108
Osborne, Thomas, 21

Paglia, Camille, 54, 101, 122, 125-26, 141
Paretsky, Sara, 154
Parke, Catherine N., 78
Parker, Hershel, 69
Pelikan, Jaroslav, 45
Percy, Thomas, 16-17
Perot, H. Ross, 65
Peyre, Henri, 10
Phelps, William Lyon, 64
Piper, William Bowman, 10
Pitt, William, 111
Plath, Sylvia, 54, 83
Plato, 20, 31, 46, 75, 96, 103
Poe, Edgar Allan, 78
Pomfret, John, 29
Pope, Alexander, 29-30, 42, 53, 80, 86, 111, 141, 144, 150, 155
Popkin, Richard, 29, 31
Porter, Katherine Anne, 51
Pound, Ezra, 23, 54
Price, Richard, 109

Priestley, J. B., 142
Prior, Matthew, 17, 100
Pryor, Richard, 103
Pynchon, Thomas, 18, 83, 99, 107-8, 126, 143

Quintilian (Marcus Fabius Quintilianus), 15

Rahner, Karl, 117
Rahv, Philip, 5
Ralegh, Walter, 140
Ransom, John Crowe, 22, 78
Raspberry, William, 67
Read, Piers Paul, 51
Rendell, Ruth, 154
Rhys, Jean, 53
Rich, Barnabe, 140
Richard, Little, 127
Richards, Keith, 128
Richardson, J. P., 126
Richardson, Samuel, 16, 53, 65, 77, 86, 104, 117, 144
Rinehart, Mary Roberts, 154
Rivera, Geraldo, 65
Robespierre, Maximilien de, 30, 96
Roosevelt, Franklin Delano, 128
Rorty, Richard, 131
Rousseau, Jean Jacques, 96-97
Rowe, Nicholas, 17
Royko, Mike, 66
Rubens, Peter Paul, 51
Runyon, Damon, 99
Rymer, Thomas, 114

Salusinszky, Imre, 85
Sandburg, Carl, 4
Sandeen, Ernest, 119
Sartre, Jean-Paul, 118, 147
Saussure, Ferdinand de, 22
Savage, Richard, 53
Sayers, Dorothy, 154
Schiller, von, Johann Christoph Friedrich, 131
Schopenhauer, Arthur, 23
Scoppettone, Sandra, 110
Scott, Sir Walter, 16

Index

Scriblerians, 29, 105
Searle, John, 134
Shakespeare, William, 12, 21, 41, 53, 86, 102, 114, 139, 145–46, 150
Shelley, Percy Bysshe, 53, 75, 78, 98
Sheridan, Richard Brinsley, 17, 107
Sherry, Norman, 141
Short, Elizabeth, 109
Sidney, Philip, 10, 13, 75, 78, 100, 106, 140
Simon, Yves, 119
Smart, Christopher, 44
Smith, Adam, 16, 43
Smith, Henry Nash, 5
Smith, Mitchell, 109
Smollett, Tobias, 16
Sowell, Thomas, 154
Spenser, Edmund, 53, 137, 139–40
Sprat, Thomas, 16
St. Clair, James, 17
Steel, Danielle, 108
Steele, Richard, 44, 53, 60, 107
Steinbeck, John, 3, 54
Steiner, George, 116
Stephens, John, 66
Sterne, Laurence, 16, 77, 104, 144
Stevens, Wallace, 54, 151
Stevenson, Robert Louis, 51
Stimpson, Catharine, 48
Stoppard, Tom, 107
Stowe, Harriet Beecher, 77
Strachey, Lytton, 54
Strahan, George, 14
Strauss, Leo, 34
Styron, William, 3, 18
Swift, Jonathan, 11, 16–17, 28–30, 42, 44, 50, 53, 104, 111, 144, 155

Tate, Allen, 22, 78
Tennyson, Alfred, Lord, 51
Thompson, Jim, 99
Thoreau, Henry D., 4, 54
Tickell, Thomas, 17
Tillyard, E. M. W., 2
Tolstoy, Leo, 108
Tompkins, Jane, 43, 84, 156
Tottel, Richard, 106
Trilling, Lionel, 5, 14, 22

Turing, Alan, 141
Turow, Scott, 108
Tusser, Thomas, 106
Twain, Mark, 70, 152

Vachss, Andrew, 99, 102, 110
Valens, Ritchie, 126
Vander Meulen, David, 121
Vida, Marco Girolamo, 15
Voegelin, Eric, 118
Voltaire (François-Marie Arouet), 54, 97, 114
Vossius, Isaac, 15

Walker, Alice, 108
Walker, John, 15
Wambaugh, Joseph, 72
Warton, Thomas, 16
Washington, George, 128
Wedgewood, Josiah, 107
Weinbrot, Howard D., 2
Weiner, Andrew, 53
Wellek, René, 90
Wells, H. G., 108
Welty, Eudora, 6
Wesley, Charles, 65
Wesley, John, 65
Wesley, Samuel, 65
West, Nathanael, 5
West, Paul, 48
Whistler, James, 6
Whitman, Walt, 4, 54
Wilde, Oscar, 54
Wilder, Thornton, 105
Wiles, Roy M., 106
Willeford, Charles, 72, 88, 93, 103, 109
Williams, Raymond, 151
Williams, Tennessee, 6, 103
Wilson, Edmund, 23, 55, 84, 96, 151
Wimsatt, William K., Jr., 68
Winchilsea, Anne Finch, Countess of, 133
Winks, Robin, 122
Winters, Yvor, 10, 22–23, 46, 87, 151
Wittgenstein, Ludwig, 42
Wolfe, Tom, 7
Wollstonecraft, Mary, 53
Woo, John, 142

Index

Woolf, Virginia, 54
Wordsworth, William, 47, 53, 97–99, 139
Wouk, Herman, 51, 108
Wright, Frank Lloyd, 4

Wright, H. Bunker, 100
Wright, Louis B., 64, 68

Yeats, William Butler, 28, 54, 102
Young, Edward, 16

Richard B. Schwartz is a professor of English and dean of the Graduate School of Arts and Sciences at Georgetown University. He has taught at the United States Military Academy and at the University of Wisconsin, Madison, where he was a professor of English and associate dean for the humanities in the Graduate School. He is the author of *Samuel Johnson and the New Science, Samuel Johnson and the Problem of Evil, Boswell's Johnson: A Preface to the* Life, *Daily Life in Johnson's London,* and a novel, *Frozen Stare,* as well as the editor of *The Plays of Arthur Murphy* and *Theory and Tradition in Eighteenth-Century Studies.*